READING

the BIBLE as if

JESUS

MATTERED

READING the BIBLE as if JESUS MATTERED

DUANE BEACHEY

Foreword by
Danny Duncan Collum

Cascadia
Publishing House
Telford, Pennsylvania

Cascadia Publishing House LLC orders, information, reprint permissions:
contact@cascadiapublishinghouse.com
1-215-723-9125
126 Klingerman Road, Telford PA 18969
www.CascadiaPublishingHouse.com

Library of Congress Cataloguing-in-Publication Data
Beachey, Duane, 1948-
Reading the Bible as if Jesus mattered / by Duane Beachey.
    pages cm
Includes bibliographical references.
Summary: "Why do Christians who are very serious about the Bible
largely ignore the words of Jesus? Exploring what might happen if Jesus
were truly our starting point, Duane Beachey tackles inerrancy, fundamentalism, creationism, the culture wars, prophesy, nationalism, materialism, war, wealth, and same-gender relations." "[summary]"-- Pro-
vided by publisher.
    ISBN 978-1-931038-99-7 (5.5 x 8.5 trade pbk. : alk. paper) -- ISBN 1-
931038-99-6 (5.5 x 8.5 trade pbk. : alk. paper)
    1. Christian life. 2. Theology, Doctrinal. I. Title.

BV4501.3.B423 2014
230--dc23

2014014941

20 11 19 18 17 16 15 14   10 9 8 7 6 5 4 3 2

"If you love me, keep my commands."
—Jesus, John 14:15

*To all those who love Jesus and
who want to love him more.*

CONTENTS

FOREWORD

The title of this book, *Reading the Bible As If Jesus Mattered,* must seem paradoxical to some. After all, aren't the life and teachings of Jesus Christ at the very center of the Bible?

Well, yes, but you can grow up and grow old in some provinces of Christendom without ever hearing very much about the life and teachings of the actual Jesus. I know that I can't remember ever hearing a sermon preached from the synoptic gospels in the Baptist congregation of my childhood and youth. The Christianity I heard proclaimed generally began and ended with Christ's vicarious atonement for our sins and the promise of life everlasting. Only a youth group Bible study on the gospel of Matthew saved me from rejecting the faith of my parents. The Sermon on the Mount opened my eyes to the person whom all the shouting was about, and I've tried to follow him ever since.

That's the experience Duane Beachey wants to provide for you, his reader. Beachey provides a clear, cogent, and engaging look at the limitations and contradictions in the fundamentalist worldview that cause many Christians either to drift away from their faith or let their faith devolve into ideology. Duane sees Christianity as, first and foremost, a matter of a lived relationship with a living person, Jesus Christ.

Duane's work is plainly evangelical. He believes in the primary authority of Scripture, seen through the prism of

God's revelation in Jesus Christ. He doesn't think Christianity is just one interesting way to approach the divine. He sees it as the truth, and he sees the reality of Jesus' life and death as the ultimate issues of history. He wants people to be or become Christians. But his preaching is also a call to action. He calls his readers to live a life that will *show* a skeptical world that Jesus lives and matters. He wants us to show this evangelical truth by living the kind of life Jesus did—one of love, self-sacrifice and mercy, especially for the poor and outcast.

Duane is a card-carrying member of the Baby Boomer generation who has held on to the idealism associated with the by-gone time of the young Boomers. To this day he lives among the poor in Appalachian southeast Kentucky, one of the most marginalized and neglected regions in the U.S. I first met him when he and his wife, Gloria, generously opened their home to my own wife and children. But, paradoxically, this makes his work especially timely because, in our twenty-first century era of endless war and struggles over human and civil rights, Jesus' message of peace and justice is coming back in style. We can see this longing for the message of Jesus in the popularity of Pope Francis, whose appeal extends far beyond his denominational fiefdom.

Among Christians in general, and especially among evangelicals, new generations ripe for the message of this book are rising. In recent decades, "Christian" in popular usage has often come to stand for a partisan political agenda that has little do with Jesus of Nazareth. But that is changing. Young evangelicals are seeking ways to get beyond the "culture wars" and sterile debates about evolution or inerrancy that have come to constitute evangelical identity.

Duane has the message that those young people are looking for. He issues a call to a radical discipleship that has always been counter-cultural and always will be. Jesus matters. He matters more than any of our customs, predilections, and prejudices. This book will help you put him back at the center of your faith.

—*Danny Duncan Collum is contributing editor and columnist for* Sojourners *magazine and professor of English and journalism at Kentucky State University.*

INTRODUCTION

The impetus for this book was seeing the wide gap between what I believe Jesus intended for his followers or disciples and how most of us actually live that out. Some of the difference is simply the result of our fallen nature—our inability to do what we believe we should. But much of the gap is caused by our not even intending to do a lot of what Jesus challenges us to do and to be. Bluntly put, we don't take Jesus' teachings seriously enough across a range of topics from poverty and wealth, to love and hate, to forgiveness, to being a servant, to taking up a cross. Jesus talked about "hearing my words and doing them" in ways that indicate *doing* is an integral part of our salvation.

One clear example of the gulf between what Jesus teaches and what the church teaches is in our understanding of salvation—who is saved and who isn't. Jesus paints a stark but straightforward picture of the judgment at the end of the age, in which the saved and unsaved are separated based on a single criterion: How did you respond to human need? "I was hungry and you fed me, thirsty and you gave me a drink. . . ."

Those who responded with compassion are told to "come . . . take their inheritance"; those who didn't are told, "Depart from me, you who are cursed" (Matt. 25:31-46). That this flies in the face of much of the church's understanding of salvation shows how little Jesus is actually our guide for belief and practice.

Yes, the Bible talks about salvation in many other ways as well, but my point is that what *Jesus* said is hardly central to the way most of us understand salvation. Belief *in* Jesus and in his death and resurrection is central to our understanding of salvation. Belief in what he taught is less so.

To be clear I don't see feeding and clothing and visiting the least of these as a new law or rule. We serve the poor because it is simply the Way of Christ—the way we love and obey God. "If you keep my commands, you will remain in my love, just as I have kept my Father's commands and remain in his love" (John 15:10). Serving the poor is the worship Jesus desires from us. When Jesus says, "Whatever you did for one of the least of these . . . you did for me," isn't he defining how we accept Christ himself?

At least two factors contribute to our not taking Jesus more seriously. First is the simple difficulty of overcoming our culture's biases, fears, and commonly held beliefs. Jesus challenges all of these. We are more comfortable deciding Jesus couldn't have meant for us to go against "common sense," which is just our culture's commonly held beliefs. Without admitting a preference for common sense rather than Jesus, we just quietly ignore much of what Jesus taught.

The second factor may depend on how we use the Bible and do our theology. Liberals talk about culture and context in a way that can make much of what Jesus says not applicable to today's world. Conservatives who claim the Bible as inerrant (without any errors) have another way of getting around Jesus. If we are in this camp, our belief in the inerrancy of all Scripture creates such a wide point of reference for understanding God's will that we can make the Bible say almost anything. Where Jesus says something that is too difficult, there will always be something more reasonable or acceptable somewhere else in the Bible. Without admitting a preference for parts of the Old Testament, or Romans, or Revelation, we simply bypass or trump Jesus.

Thus a part of this book is my own attempt to see the Bible with Jesus as the central revelation from God. I find a different understanding of Scripture when I start with Jesus, the Word made flesh, and try to understand everything else in light of his perspective and his life among us. Much of this book is a critique of how we miss Jesus, but the final chapter is how I understand the good news of the kingdom of God that Jesus constantly talked about. So if the first ten chapters seem like too much bad news, read the last for the good news.

Having laid out my reasons for writing this book, the question still remains—why should you read it? Most Christians would not admit or accept that we don't follow Jesus. We certainly intend to. We just haven't thought about our lives in much detail as it relates to what Jesus taught except in general terms—to be loving and forgiving to the extent that common sense allows.

If you're willing to be challenged to take a deeper look at how Jesus words might apply to your life, you can explore that with me. If you sense that Jesus has little real power in your life, you may need to take his words more seriously— even more literally. If you see as I do that the church seems to have been swallowed up by our culture, we will look at that as well.

Maybe you find yourself agreeing with the church's critics about the terrible things that have been done in the name of Christ and the hypocrisy within the church. Might the problem be that we have taken Jesus too lightly? Jesus questioned the very foundation of the faith of the religious folks of his day—the folks who were so sure they understood the Scriptures and *were* taking them seriously.

I realize many people hesitate ever to question their faith for fear of questioning God. They assume that what they have always believed and been taught *is* orthodox and fundamental to Christian faith, and they just want to stick to those simple fundamentals. Evangelicals especially are committed to taking their Christian faith seriously, but too often they don't sound much like the Jesus they proclaim. Maybe they aren't asking *enough* of the tough questions.

I hope to raise questions in your mind about Christian beliefs and practices, not to weaken your faith but to strengthen it. The Psalms are filled with questions and even doubts about God, yet the Psalmist always reaffirms his faith in God. The reformer Martin Luther challenged over a thousand years of Christian orthodoxy, and we are all (including Catholics) the better for it. You don't have to be a theologian or academic to question what is accepted or believed by nearly everyone. In this particular case you may just need to keep asking the simple question WWJD?—what would Jesus do?

I write this with the assumption

> that it is reasonable to follow Jesus daily . . . practical to live by the Sermon on the Mount and the whole New Testament literally, honestly, sacrificially . . . thinkable to practice the way of reconciling love in [all] human conflicts . . . possible to confess Jesus as Lord above all nationalisms, racism, or materialism . . . feasible to build a [community of believers] mutually committed to each other in Christ . . . a life lived simply, following the Jesus-way in lifestyle, in possessions, in service. (David Augsburger)

Perhaps you haven't really questioned or thought that much about how your Christian faith affects your daily life, and have just taken for granted that you pretty much understand what it means to be a Christian. On the other hand, you may think your faith should have more depth or meaning than it does. Maybe you are already asking questions about your Christian faith, or maybe even questions about Christianity itself.

Wherever you find yourself along that continuum, if you are like many Christians, including myself, you have this nagging sense that Jesus must have intended a lot more of us, and *for* us, than we are experiencing or living in the church today. Although we are often blinded by the familiar, we catch glimpses of what Jesus may be trying to show us. A crisis or a new experience can pull us away from the familiar and open our eyes to see what we never noticed before in our lives.

Let me give you an example. Those of us in the United States or Canada live in wealthy countries with homes, cars, food, and clothes for nearly everyone. Our stuff surrounds us.

It is the background noise and "wallpaper" of our lives. Most of us never think about all our stuff and just assume there is nothing wrong with any of it. If anything, we believe it is an example of the way God has blessed us. But send any college student for a year or a semester or even a short mission trip to Guatemala or Zimbabwe, and her or his horizon is suddenly expanded. Such students find Christian brothers and sisters living with much less, yet grateful for all of God's blessings, who share more freely and generously than most of the people they know. Students ask new questions like, "Who has God really blessed?"

Their eyes are opened a second time on returning home and really *seeing* for the first time all the stuff we have and consume and throw away and destroy. Why do we have so much? Is it a sign of God's blessing or of our own greed? For the first time their lives seem so wrong—even obscene. Some will squeeze what they've experienced back into a context that fits North American realities and worldviews. They will soon fit back into the life they had before and mostly forget what was so obvious. Others may not so easily shake their new insight. It may affect the rest of their lives. They may never again quite feel comfortable within materialistic cultures. I believe they have seen with Jesus' eyes of compassion.

Throughout this book I make repeated references to the Pharisees, because I see parallels between these establishment religious leaders and the church today. My references to Pharisees tend to reflect the generally negative perceptions of the gospel writers regarding Jesus' ongoing conflict with these religious leaders and teachers. I realize this conflict did not apparently include all Pharisees. The Gospels at various points indicate at least some Pharisees looked favorably on Jesus.

Two factors I should note regarding this conflict: first, the Gospels were written after Judaism and the Christian community had become alienated from each other. Christians were no longer welcome to speak in the synagogues. The Gospels reflect this alienation.

Second, this conflict between Jesus and the Pharisees and teachers and religious leaders of his day is repeated at many other times and places when visionaries and charismatic leaders arise and challenge any religious establishment. I don't believe the Pharisees were uniquely stubborn, suspicious, or judgmental but rather that, as viewed by the Gospel writers, they exemplify the rather ordinary tendency of established religious leaders to respond defensively to new ideas—even attempting at times to destroy the prophets in their midst.

The tragedy of the Pharisees in Jesus' time as the New Testament portrays them was that they were so dedicated to following God's Law but didn't see with eyes of compassion. They missed God's visitation on the day of his coming. They didn't just miss recognizing their Messiah. They missed him because they didn't recognize the God that Jesus knew so intimately. The God that Jesus talked about didn't fit their understanding of God. For all their study of God's Word, they missed the One to whom it pointed—they missed God's most important Word. They weren't willing and didn't think they needed to rethink the core of their belief.

I fear that tragedy is repeating itself among us today. I only hope to raise a question in the hearts of those who sincerely seek to follow Jesus.

READING

the **BIBLE** *as if*

JESUS

MATTERED

Chapter One

SEARCHING THE SCRIPTURES AND MISSING JESUS

"You study the Scriptures diligently because you think that in them you have eternal life. These are the very Scriptures that testify about me, yet you refuse to come to me to have life."
—John 5: 39-40

"You are free to eat from any tree in the garden; but you must not eat from the tree of the knowledge of good and evil, for when you eat from it you will certainly die."
—Genesis 2: 16-17

I found that the very commandment that was intended to bring life actually brought death.
—Romans 7: 10

If there is one thing most Christians intend, it is to take the Bible very seriously. We might not have the bumper sticker that says, "The Bible says it, I believe it, and that settles it," but it's our philosophy. Scripture is everything, and we believe all of it from Genesis to Revelation.

In Jesus' time the Pharisees also studied the Scriptures diligently. They believed in an afterlife for the righteous and were very intent on fulfilling God's requirements for eternal life. They searched the Scriptures to attain eternal life, Jesus says, but they missed the most important thing in all their study of Scripture. They missed the Christ to whom the Scriptures pointed.

The Pharisees were serious about studying the Scriptures and putting them into practice in their daily lives. They studied all the prophecies about the coming Messiah. They were so certain of their interpretations that even when they saw the blind given sight, the lame walking, and the demon-possessed delivered, most of them were not convinced. The common people and even prostitutes and tax collectors believed, but the scholars of Scripture missed "God with us."

The Pharisees were sincere in their faith and practice but often sincerely wrong. They were wrong about the reach of God's love and grace, wrong about the priority God places on religious practices—even those commanded by Scripture, wrong about what constitutes true righteousness, and wrong about the prophesied Messiah even though they spent endless hours studying prophecy. They were so wrong that when the Messiah stood before them, they didn't recognize him.

Jesus wasn't as serious as they were about keeping the Law, particularly the Sabbath laws and the purification laws. He was too friendly with sinners, prostitutes, tax collectors, Samaritans, and Gentiles—he accepted and forgave them too easily. Most of all, he didn't fulfill prophesies about the Messiah as they understood them. Jesus' message and method—the way of the cross—ran so counter to the way the Pharisees read the Scripture that they rejected Jesus as their Messiah. It just didn't fit what they were so sure they understood from the Scripture.

We know that at least a few Pharisees did accept Jesus. They heard his message and believed, but for most Pharisees, what Jesus taught about God's priorities never fit well with their understanding or expectations because they were so contrary to their common beliefs. Repeatedly in Matthew 5, Jesus says, "You have heard . . . but I tell you . . . " as he reinterprets the Law. He challenges the Pharisees' prejudices, their judgments of other people, their elevated social status, their stored up wealth, their lack of concern for the poor, their hatred for the Roman occupiers, their scriptural understanding, and especially their understanding of God, and God's priorities. In all those areas, Jesus challenges us too. He challenges our common beliefs and at times even our "common sense."

Should we take a second look at Jesus' conflict with the Pharisees and ask questions of ourselves? My intention is not to pick a fight, or to be derogatory about many sincere, good, and dedicated Christians who are seeking to be faithful to God and his word. However, when I read what Jesus said about and to other sincere religious folks who were trying to hold the line against sin and against the sinners of their day, I can't help but see parallels. Does the clash between Jesus and the religious folks of his day have something important to say to us today? Are *we* searching the Scriptures as the Pharisees did, but missing the Jesus they point to?

Jesus says of the Pharisees, "Nor does [the Father's] word dwell in you, for you do not believe the one he sent" (John 5:38).

What is Jesus getting at? Is he saying if the Pharisees would only accept him as the Christ—the Messiah of Israel—then they would have eternal life? No, because another time he also says, "Why do you call me, 'Lord, Lord,' and do not *do* what I say (Luke 6:46)? "Therefore everyone who hears my words and *puts them into practice* is like a wise man who built his house on the rock" (Matt. 7:24-27 emph. added). He also said not everyone who *calls* him Lord will enter the kingdom of Heaven but only those who *do* the Father's will (Matt. 7:21).

In his Great Commission, Jesus tells his followers to go into the whole world preaching the good news, baptizing new followers, and teaching them to *obey* everything he commanded (Matt. 28:19-20). Jesus consistently emphasizes the importance of actually doing what he taught, not just confessing belief in him.

The Heart of Compassion

The God revealed to us in Jesus is a God of love and compassion. Even God's judgment, according to Jesus, is reserved for those who *lacked* love and compassion. He described a judgment scene where the saved and unsaved are separated based on their response to those in need—"I was hungry, thirsty, unclothed, sick, in prison," then he adds that whatever our response, he takes it personally. Jesus repeated this basis of judgment with the fate of the rich man who ignored poor Lazarus. Over and over Jesus was moved with compassion for those he met. The way he cared for people was always his priority over the way the Pharisees understood the Law.

The Pharisees started from the wrong place. They thought the words of Scripture were the highest priority for being a holy and godly people. Jesus lived out of a different center. Love and compassion for people always took priority in the way he understood Scriptures regarding the Sabbath, adultery, forgiveness, or any other Scripture. To be clear, Jesus didn't downplay the Law. He simply understood all the Law and the Prophets to be hung on the twin principles of love for God and love for neighbor (Matt. 22:37-40). Anything that didn't demonstrate those two mandates was a misunderstanding of God's will and God's Law.

For Jesus, loving people took priority over any other religious observances, rules, or doctrines. Actually the foundational doctrine, observance, or rule is the rule of love. The people Jesus spoke harshly about were those who didn't put loving people first—those who instead gave priority to the Law—which in truth was their own interpretation of the Law, which was always compromised by their position and status and wealth. Wasn't that why Jesus said that unless our righteousness exceeds that of the Pharisees, we can't enter the Reign of Heaven?

Jesus criticized Pharisees who dedicated a portion of their wealth to God and then couldn't take care of their parents in their old age (Matt. 15:3-6, Mark 7:9-13). While they were thinking of their religious duties, Jesus was thinking about their duty to the people closest to them. The priority

for the Pharisees was just being sure they obeyed the requirements of the Law. They were all about keeping the Law in
every detail. Their salvation depended on it. They discussed
and debated every angle of the Law until they had it nailed
down.

NOT JUST A MUSHY FEEL-GOOD ETHIC

Many Christians today have that same desire to nail
things down. They don't want some mushy ethic of "do
whatever feels good now." They need to know that God's
laws are eternal truths, that they stand for all time—and that
we can know such truths. By these truths we can be sure of
our own standing with God. Of course we will also know
that others are not in good standing with God, *if* they have
not done or believed what we know is necessary to be right
with God.

Not only did the Pharisees know they were right, they
also knew others were wrong. Because they were so certain
about the Law's requirements, they held themselves above
the ordinary sinners they felt were below them. It was this
certainty about what the Scriptures said that blinded the
Pharisees to God in their midst.

Paul, also a Pharisee, must have been keenly aware of
how utterly wrong he was about the very things of which he
had been *so sure* he was right. When he met the risen Christ
he had to do a complete turn-around. All his study of Scripture and his confidence in his understanding of Scripture
had only blinded him to what God was doing in his time.
Paul says the commandments that were intended to bring
life actually brought death. For Paul specifically his depending on the Law (or his interpretation of the Law) led him in
the wrong direction. More generally he saw the Law leading
people away from a life lived under the grace of God. To
know the Law doesn't bring with it the ability to *keep* the
Law. So Paul says we are left under judgment for knowing
the Law but not being able to keep it. Knowing the Law
didn't bring his faith to life.

KNOWING GOOD FROM EVIL—LIKE GOD

The story in Genesis of how sin first came into the world includes this same theme—that eating from the "tree of the knowledge of good and evil" brought death into the world. Isn't that what the Law is? The knowledge of good and evil? The story in Genesis suggests that the temptation was ultimately the temptation to *be like God, knowing good and evil"* (Gen. 3:5). This brings with it the temptation to take another of God's prerogatives—to judge others.

The irony of those making the case for absolute or eternal truths is that the issues nearly always involve some moral concern which someone else sees differently. So the argument for eternal truths is often more of an argument about our being right than a statement of God's eternal nature. If we are right, then others are wrong—and sinful. In that context "faith" becomes arrogance—*knowing* we are right and claiming for ourselves absolute truth. Instead of faith meaning trust in God, even when we can't see clearly, our faith becomes the certainty that we know definitely what God wants. Our "faith" is ultimately in our own "knowledge of good and evil," which is itself the root of our sin and brokenness.

I believe our need for absolute truths should be replaced by faith in a God who can be absolutely trusted because only God has absolute truth, whereas we often "see through a glass darkly," and we know only in part (1 Cor. 13:12 KJV). Paul's assertion that "We live by faith, not by sight" (2 Cor. 5:7), suggests our faith is only exercised when we realize we don't see clearly.

There was another tree in the garden—the "tree of life." When we live our lives under the Spirit's direction, we depend on a living faith to guide us. Even though there may be many things we cannot know, Jesus promises that the Holy Spirit will lead us into all truth (John 16:12-13).

JESUS THE SOURCE OF TRUTH

Jesus said "the way, the truth, and the life" reside in him. He even claimed authority over the Law, repeating, "You have heard it said . . . but I tell you. . . ." He wasn't just saying, "It's been said . . . " or "Some people say . . . " but rather he was saying that Scripture says, . . . but this is what I say. Because every example he gives is actually a passage from the Torah Law that he restates (Matt. 5:21, 27, 31, 33, 38, 43).

He claimed knowledge about God's will above the written Law when he said of the Torah that Moses allowed divorce because of the hardness of Israel's heart but from the beginning that wasn't what God wanted (Mark 10:4-6). Can you imagine if teachers today claimed to have authority over the Scripture? No matter what miracles they performed, would churches today accept them? Wouldn't we also judge them blasphemers?

Again and again Jesus valued people over the Law. When he said, "The Sabbath was made for man, not man for the Sabbath," he could as well have said, "The Law was made for man, not man for the Law." At any point that the Law didn't fit Jesus' understanding of love for God and neighbor, Jesus restated the Law, saying, "But I say. . . ."

Isn't Jesus the final and primary standard for all his followers? All other authorities or revelations or Scripture are tested against him. Jesus said if you have seen him you have seen what God is like, you've "seen the Father" (John 14:9). Although we can continue to learn much from those who view matters differently, the Christian understanding is that Jesus completed the Old Testament Scriptures, not just in fulfilling prophesies about him but also in the sense of bringing to fullness or perfecting the Old Testament revelation of God. Jesus was and is the final word from and about God—God's Word perfected and brought to fullness, or fulfilled.

THE BROAD AND THE NARROW WAY

The Way of Christ, though grounded in love, is hardly an open-ended or permissive way. He says the road to destruction is wide and many will follow it, while the road to life is narrow and few will take it (Matt. 7:13-14).

What is he saying? If the narrow way includes all who have made a confession of faith in Jesus, the road isn't very narrow at all. Many have taken that road. In some areas of the country and in some countries the majority of the population has made the confession. If we try to narrow it down by judging which people's confessions are sincere or which church's confession is the correct confession, we simply end up arguing over doctrines.

Is it safe to assume Jesus wasn't talking about a confession of faith at all, but a way of life that few will follow? Jesus had a lot to say about those who say the right words but don't live them out. He tells of two sons whose father asked them both to work in the fields. One said sure he would do it but then didn't get around to it; the other said no but then felt bad about his response and went ahead and did the work. Which one, Jesus asked, did the Father's will? Of course the response was—the one who actually did it (Matt. 21: 28-32). Confessions are easy to make. With the support and urging of a church community, even very public confessions aren't that difficult or embarrassing. Following Jesus in life is tougher.

What is the wide way—the one nearly everyone is on? Isn't it the way of self-interest, self-gratification, self-preservation? Isn't the narrow way the way of self-sacrifice to others and self-surrender to the will of God?

THE WAY OF CHRIST AND THE WAY OF LOVE

Taking Jesus rather than something else from the Law or other Scripture as our ultimate authority gives us then two standards of truth by which we can live our lives or "test the Scripture," as the Bereans did (Acts 17:11). We aren't simply left to our own wisdom, or whatever seems right to us. We are held to two standards—the way of Christ, and the way of love for God and neighbor, against which all else is tested and understood. In truth, it is *one* test, because to live out of the heart of Christ *is* to live out of a heart of love for God and neighbor. This is not a dangerously subjective criterion, either for testing the Scripture or for living our lives. This is neither us doing whatever seems right in our own eyes nor depending on our own works of righteousness for our salvation.

By this point many Christians will have become quite uneasy about all this talk of "doing" all that Jesus taught. Isn't this just another form of law or works righteousness?

There is a great deal of misunderstanding about grace and "works" related to Jesus' criticism of the Pharisees. We have understood the Pharisees to have depended on their righteousness and goodness to save them. Jesus says that unless our righteousness exceeds that of the Pharisees we cannot enter into the reign of heaven (Matt. 5:20). But weren't the Pharisees scrupulously righteous? So how can we expect to outdo them? The answer is usually thought to be only through the righteousness imputed to us by believing in Jesus. The problem with this understanding is that is has little to do with how we live our lives and only to do with a change in what we believe or confess about Jesus. How we actually live is irrelevant to our salvation in this understanding.

The second problem is that it isn't Jesus' priority. He never endorsed a faith not demonstrated with real action born out of love. The problem wasn't that the Pharisees depended on being righteous but that they depended on being religious. Their zeal wasn't to show great compassion and mercy to the least of these. That would have been true righteousness. Their zeal went into obeying the Law scrupulously—the Sabbath laws, the cleanliness laws, tithing laws, sacrificial laws, and just studying the Law endlessly for its own sake. Most of that had little to do with God's real concerns of justice and mercy and faithfulness (Matt. 23:23). In the process of keeping the rules of the Law, they lost the core of the Law—to love God and neighbor.

In short, we never hear a single word or suggestion from Jesus or any other biblical writer that true compassion and mercy to the poor or hungry can become a form of "works righteousness" overshadowing faith in Jesus. Christian writers today try to make that point as though even works of compassion can be a trap. The Bible never does. James suggests that such "works" are a demonstration of our faith (James 2:14-26).

Paul says that even if he gave away all he possessed to feed the poor and didn't have *love* it would be worthless (1

Cor. 13:3). He doesn't say, " but do not have faith." He ends that chapter saying that we are left finally with faith, hope, and love—and that the greatest of these three is *love*. In much of the church today we hear that the most important thing is faith.

WHAT IS THE SALVATION MESSAGE?

In most of the evangelistic sermons I've heard, the emphasis is primarily on our confession and putting our faith in Jesus. Faith, in this context has been reduced to what we believe, rather than meaning faithfulness and obedience. We believe *in* Jesus, rather than believing and living what he taught. Jesus preached about the reign of God and a forgiving Father, but he expected his followers to live changed lives that demonstrated real "fruit" (Matt. 7:16-21).

When a man questioned Jesus on what was required to inherit eternal life, Jesus told him to keep the twin commandments—to love God with his whole heart, and to love his neighbor as himself. *"Do this,"* he said, *"and you will live."* Wanting a more specific answer the man asked, "And who is my neighbor?" and Jesus told the story of the good Samaritan. The point of the story is that eternal life entails real acts of mercy (Luke 10:25-37).

We preach of God's forgiveness and grace being free if we first confess our sins, but Jesus says God's forgiveness and grace hinges on our willingness to forgive others (Matt. 6:15). The prayer he taught us even asks God to forgive our sins *as* we forgive others.

At times Jesus forgives sins of people who haven't even requested forgiveness. When a paralyzed man is brought to him for healing, he tells the man his sins are forgiven and that he should get up and walk (Matt. 9:2, Mark 2:5). And to Zacchaeus, who promises to give half his wealth to the poor and to return fourfold all the money he cheated out of people, Jesus declares, "Today salvation has come to this house" (Luke 19:9). Salvation follows acts of true repentance and turning in a new direction—toward Christ and his Way. Which brings us back to the way of love.

While the Pharisees were judging others and saying, "But the Scripture says . . . " compassion for people's pain was moving Jesus. The Pharisees were so intent on studying the Scriptures but they missed the whole point.

Whenever our *understanding* of Scripture diminishes or contradicts the Jesus of Scripture, or if it doesn't reflect the love of God revealed in Christ, then we too have missed the whole point of the Scriptures—which is to point us to the way, the truth, and the life embodied in the person of Jesus. There is no other way to God than the *Way* of Christ, the *truth* he taught, and the *life* he calls us to (John 14:6).

LOSING YOUR LIFE TO SAVE IT

If our first priority is to follow Jesus, can we just follow his teachings in a literal way and enter into God's reign? We might like to, but Jesus' words don't lend themselves to rules or formulas for living. His words are stories, parables, poetry. Should we give all of our money to the poor, and be poor ourselves? No, that is more categorical than Jesus usually was. But we are to love our neighbor as ourselves, and not horde our wealth—in short hold it loosely and let it go easily, knowing that God loves us deeply and can be trusted with the question. If we lived accordingly, what would happen to us?

The same assurance underlies Jesus' call to turn the other cheek; and we want to ask, "What would happen to us if we all did that?" Wouldn't people just run over us? The answer to that question is to ask, "Did anyone run over Jesus?" Our fear of taking Jesus seriously is really tied to that central question—What would happen to us? Because we don't know if God can really be trusted or if he will love us enough.

Over and over Jesus says two things. *"O, ye of little faith,"* and *"Fear not."* Jesus is absolutely convinced of God's love and care for us. Most of our sin is because we don't know if we can actually trust God that much. So we keep trying to make ourselves secure with material things or through force and violence. Our lying and cheating and stealing and killing are all based on our need to take care of our own security and power. Our gossiping and meanness and bitterness are the same—destroying the other person before they destroy us. Don't we do all that to protect ourselves from destruction or loss—actually from death? Our fear of death and our need for control is at the root of our sin and brokenness, isn't it?

Jesus calls us to lay our lives down. We save our life by losing it—or just letting go of our life and letting go of our need for control. Jesus' resurrection proves him right and assures us that his way of letting it all go is ultimately safe. So we are freed to follow the seemingly risky way of letting go to share freely, forgive constantly, and love indiscriminately—not as a set of rules but as our guiding principles for life.

At one point in Jesus' ministry many of his followers were leaving him because of some difficult things he said. He turned to his disciples and asked if they would leave as well, and Peter replied, "Lord, to whom shall we go? You have the words of eternal life" (John 6:66-68). Jesus calls us to forsake all and follow him. We aren't called to follow a new set of rules but to follow the risen Lord wherever that leads us. Through it all we are to love God with all we have and all we are and our neighbor (whoever needs us) as ourselves.

JESUS SEES YOU

Most of my life I've worked in low-income neighborhoods repairing homes for the elderly and disabled. A woman called me one day to fix her floor that had some rotten boards that were falling through. I went and looked at it. She had a hardwood oak floor with no subfloor. In two or three places boards had broken through. The family had nailed some scraps of plywood on top which were catching her walker and wheelchair. She was an amputee.

I went and got a few pieces of hardwood and my tools and came back to do a simple job that I thought would take a couple of hours. I pried up the first patch and cut out the broken board. When I looked through the hole I had made in the floor I saw six inches of water standing under the house.

There was barely twelve inches of crawl space between the joists and the ground and half of that was full of water.

I groaned inwardly. The job had just gotten a lot worse. I was tempted to just fix the hole and leave it. But once you've seen a problem that big, you can't just leave it. Since there was no room to get under the house, I got a flashlight and a mirror from the woman and shone the light and used the mirror to look around.

I found that the drain line from the washer had broken loose about fifteen feet away under the bathroom where it hooked to the sewer. So every time she did her laundry, the washer was dumping all the water under the house.

I informed the woman and told her the only thing I could do was to cut another hole through her vinyl bathroom floor, fix the pipe, and put the piece of floor back in the hole. She said to go ahead. When I had patched the drain pipe and was ready to close the floor back up, I called the woman into the bathroom to see how I had fixed it. She hopped in on her one leg and a walker and looked down the hole at the repaired drain and at all the water under her house. She just shook her head and said what a miracle it was that the leak had been discovered before it destroyed her foundation and house.

Then she looked straight at me and made the sign of the cross like a priest giving someone a blessing and she simply said, "Jesus sees you. Jesus sees you."

I'd been doing this kind of work for over twenty years and often my "ministry" seemed just a job, but her affirmation and reminder—her blessing—brought tears to my eyes. I felt God wanted to remind me what I was about and whose I was.

Sometimes I read or hear something that sticks with me for a long time and really impacts my life. I just can't remember years later where I heard it. This is one of those thoughts: *There isn't any question that God deeply loves every single person we will ever encounter; the only question is if God will be able to love each of them through us.*

Chapter Two

LIVING AS FUNCTIONAL ATHEISTS

I read Sam Harris' book, *Letter to a Christian Nation*. Harris is among contemporary atheists who have authored books to convince people of atheist beliefs. It's an interesting book. He's right about some things. I'd have to say that I couldn't believe in some of the descriptions of God he offers either. He highlights the worst abuses of people of faith and blames the religion itself for those abuses. He points out Christians who burned heretics at the stake and Muslims who are terrorists then says both were actually taking their sacred texts literally. Therefore religion itself is the problem.

Indeed he is right that when people of any religion use their religion to justify crusades or inquisitions or terrorism, the results are atrocities. Harris correctly emphasizes that much of what we've done in the name of Christianity (and Islam) hasn't been very loving or kind.

Indeed as has often been pointed out, if we took literally biblical commands from the God of the Old Testament, we would still be stoning disobedient children, the adulterous, and the infidel. But Christians today, and Jews for that matter, are pretty much unanimous in rejecting such punishments. We don't feel such biblical mandates should still be practiced.

That leaves us with the problem of how to understand these passages from our shared spiritual past. Were the early Israelites misguided? Was theirs the normal justice of an earlier time? Was God stricter under Torah law than under grace? Was their view of God incomplete and imperfect? Or were they just plain wrong about what God wanted?

These questions of how to understand our Scriptures go to the heart of our faith understandings, which is why disagreements about Scripture are some of the most difficult and divisive. I'll say more in a later chapter about how we understand Scripture.

Muslims also disagree on how to understand similar harsh punishments in the Koran. Like Christians and Jews, many Muslims today do not believe such punishments should still be carried out—though it seems more Muslims than Christians or Jews still embrace the harsh penalties prescribed in *sharia* law based on their Scriptures.

Much of Sam Harris' argument is still the original philosophical standoff that says you can't *prove* God exists and the counter argument that you can't prove God *doesn't* exist. While Christians may look at the complexity and beauty of creation and see that as proof of God's existence, Harris looks at all the tragedy and disease in the natural world and sees those as proof that a loving God could never have designed such a brutal unfeeling universe.

Some of Harris' critiques of Christianity need to be taken seriously. I think he points out some of the problems with the religious beliefs we have attached to Christianity. In an interview with Sam Harris and Rick Warren in the April 9, 2007 *Newsweek*, Harris asks how it is fair "to have created a [religious] system where belief is the crucial piece, rather than being a good person?" Rick Warren doesn't contest this characterization of Christianity (p. 63). In fact, Jesus insists that belief or confession of him as Lord, without obedience to his teaching, is useless.

I thought Harris had some interesting observations about belief and unbelief. He makes the point that *most* of us are atheists and non-believers—in relation to the faith of other people. Christians don't look at the Koran and believe

it is God's Word at all. Most would believe it is just a book
written by Mohammad; it may contain some wisdom and
truth but also passages we would take issue with. Most
Christians would feel the same way about the wisdom of
Buddha or the Book of Mormon. We don't believe God inspired them at all and may wonder how anyone could.

In the same way Muslims are atheists in relation to much
of the New Testament. They may also claim Abraham as
their father and see the Torah but not much of the New Testament as revealed Word. They may well claim Jesus as a mes-
senger from God who preceded Mohammad, but they don't
see passages about Jesus as Son of God or his death and resurrection as God's Word at all.

I was speaking to a Muslim at an interfaith dialogue and
was surprised when he said, "As Jesus himself once said,
. . . " and proceeded to quote Jesus saying something I'd
never heard in my life. Turns out it was a quote from the
Koran which says that Jesus said those words. I don't remember at all what he said but do recall wondering why
anyone would go to the Koran for quotes from Jesus. Of
course the reason is obvious; we each have different sources
of authority. He believed the Koran has authority, and I believe the Bible does.

While Sam Harris may be right that most of us don't believe the scriptures of the other, he didn't convince me that
there is therefore no true religion, no authoritative book, and
no God. I'm sure he also hasn't convinced many Muslims of
that, or Mormons, Buddhists, or Hindus either. We are not
easily moved from our beliefs, especially our religious beliefs. Those things we believe to be ultimately true are often
the most unshakeable. It takes a lot to pry us loose enough
even to question our beliefs, let alone change them. For the
apostle Paul it took a blinding light and the voice of Jesus to
change what he was absolutely sure he was right about.

DO WE ALL NEED A BLINDING LIGHT?

When I realized how ineffectual all of Harris' logical arguments were in shaking what I believe about God, I saw the

difficulty in what I was trying to do, which is to get Christians to think differently about things that go to the very core of their faith. Some Christians believe things that seem impossible even to other Christians, but to those who believe, such things seem absolutely orthodox. People are not easily shaken from their faith.

Lewis Carroll mocked the faith in the impossible held by the Mad Hatter in *Alice in Wonderland*. When Alice said something was impossible, he responded that he could easily believe six impossible things before breakfast. But is that faith? To profess belief in the impossible? Can we really believe one thing in our "real world" life and believe the opposite at a faith level? And if so, what does that mean?

A friend of mine, though not a Catholic, was trying to convince me that the Catholic belief in trans-substantiation was true—that in the Eucharist, the bread and wine *actually* become the body and blood of Jesus. I asked if that meant we could take the bread and wine once they were consecrated and view them under a microscope and see the red corpuscles of the blood and the cells of a human body. No, he said, but they still are actually the body and blood to eyes of faith.

But I asked what it even means to say something is actually true when it isn't *actually* true. I guess it is in some way actually spiritually true, but it's still not actually physically true. Yet such beliefs are not easily shaken for those who believe them, since there is no physical or logical way to prove or disprove them.

Maybe it goes to the heart of all our attempts to touch the transcendent. Donald Miller in his book *Blue Like Jazz* says,

> It comforts me to think that if we are created beings, the thing that created us would have to be far greater than us. . . . It would have to be greater than the facts of our reality, and so it would seem to us, looking out from within our reality, that it would contradict reason. (p. 201)

Isn't that the nature of faith—choosing to believe in what we cannot see or know because there is something beyond ourselves and beyond all seeing and knowing? The wonder of the Christian faith is the belief that in Jesus the transcendent was in fact seen and known.

Muslims place their ultimate faith in Allah as revealed in the Koran; Jews in the God known in the Torah; Mormons in the *Book of Mormon* as well as the Bible. Modernist Christian scholars may believe in Jesus, but their belief in reason and scientific inquiry often hold the final word in what they can believe about him. So they end up with more faith in science and reason than in the biblical documents themselves.

Evangelical Christians can believe in the Bible in a way that just as effectively neutralizes Jesus. I mentioned this in my introduction, but let me explain more fully what I mean. I'm not a fundamentalist or a literalist about the Bible, but I don't have a problem with people who are, *if* they are also literalists about the words of Jesus—sometimes called "red letter Christians" in reference to Bibles with the words of Jesus printed in red. Followers of Jesus should treat his words as the first place to take a firm stand. If Jesus is Lord, his words have the highest priority. If Christians want to take the Bible seriously or even literally, they can hardly have a conservative and literal view of Genesis and Revelation, then ignore or explain away the words of Jesus.

But many Christians have such a high view of the whole Bible that it's pretty easy to find other parts of "God's word" through which to neutralize much of what Jesus taught. For example (and I'll elaborate in a later chapter) if you tell most Christians that we should love our enemies rather than kill them, they will jump into all the war stories of the Old Testament to show that sometimes God commands us to kill our enemies. Or they go to Romans 13 to justify governments and their wars. So you see we don't really need to take Jesus literally when it comes to loving our enemies; in fact Jesus couldn't have meant *those* enemies. Much of the Bible seems a lot more practical than Jesus, so it's pretty easy to find something else we're more comfortable with.

JESUS *IS* THE BLINDING LIGHT!

And here is why I am hopeful that some of us may consider rethinking our faith understandings. I believe we Christians agree on the centrality of Christ to the Christian faith. The central belief of the Christian faith is that the transcendent God is made known to us most fully in Jesus who lived and taught among us—who we heard and saw with our own eyes, and who our hands have touched (1 John 1:1). The One who is beyond all seeing and knowing has become visible and is made known in Jesus the Christ:

> The Son is the image of the invisible God, the first-born over all creation. For in him all things were created: things in heaven and on earth, visible and invisible, whether thrones or powers or rulers or authorities; all things have been created through him and for him. He is before all things, and in him all things hold together. (Col. 1:15-17)

Everything fits together in Jesus alone. Nothing trumps Jesus. All that I am and have—all my belongings, all my relationships, all my beliefs, my philosophies, my politics, and especially my understanding of God and the Bible—all are subservient to Jesus. All kings and governing authorities are subservient to him. The Christian confession of the early church, "Jesus is Lord," stood in direct opposition to Rome's claim, "Caesar is Lord." Paul is clear that we can pledge no other allegiance nor have any higher authority, because *everything* else is subservient to Jesus.

We can only truly understand the words of Scripture in light of the words of Jesus. But over and over Christians explain Jesus in light of some other part of the Bible. Or we just allow our "common sense"—the world's wisdom—to convince us we can't possibly do what Jesus says or that he didn't mean what he taught in any way that actually applies to our current situation.

As Christians, we would like to think we have a fundamentally different view of reality from atheists like Sam Harris. But do we really live all that differently in our everyday lives? In his book *Let Your Life Speak*, Parker Palmer says we are often functional atheists. We believe "that ultimate responsibility for everything rests with us" (p. 88). Often we put our faith in God only when we are at the very end of our rope. Most of us Christians live our everyday lives as if God didn't exist. By that I mean, the practical and pragmatic as well as the impulsive decisions we make every day are pretty much based on the same criteria used by non-believers.

As a result Christians aren't living much different or better lives than non-Christians. According to some polls, divorce, domestic abuse, sexual abuse, pre-marital sex, sexual affairs, and other moral indicators are as high inside the church as outside. More to the point, our lives don't look much like Jesus.

Like the Pharisees of Jesus' day, many of us Christians claim we have committed our whole lives to God, but in practical matters we allow the world's wisdom to guide our lives. We believe in Christ as a spiritual truth—a sacrifice for our sins that assures us a place in the next life—but we don't believe he can be followed in this one.

I don't want to diminish the importance of Jesus' death and resurrection to our forgiveness and salvation. But neither Jesus nor the apostles suggest we can claim his forgiveness and receive him as Lord unless we actually follow him as Lord and master. Calling him "Lord" implies obedience. Are we building on the rock of living as he taught—"Who hears these words of mine and puts them into practice" (Matt. 7:24-27)? Or are we building on shifting sands that will not stand the test?

What *does* our Christian faith mean? Is it making us better people—kinder people, more forgiving, more generous, more faithful, more honest—in short, more Christ-like? Jesus says, "By their fruit you will recognize them" (Matt. 7:16). Ultimately how we live our lives speaks louder than anything we say as to what we really believe and where we truly have placed our faith.

Chapter Three

THE DEEPER CULTURE WAR

Some Christian leaders are writing and speaking about a "culture war" in America. They are trying to combat the loose morals and values of the secular culture with Christian values. For some, the concern seems to be holding the line or enforcing Christian morality on the larger secular culture. They aspire to use the power of the state to enforce their own Christian values.

Others are simply concerned that the morals of the secular culture are creeping into the church. Marriages are crumbling, teens are adopting the styles and entertainment of the surrounding culture, homosexuality is being accepted as normative within mainline churches, and personal happiness is an end in itself. In an interview about his book, *Grace Gone Wild*, Robert Jeffress said, "There is little or no discernible lifestyle difference between Christians and non-Christians. I believe we are using grace as a cover, as a license to sin" (*Christianity Today*, March, 2006, 76).

I suggest the problem goes far deeper than the concerns of most of the "culture war" writers and speakers. The culture has co-opted us to a far greater degree than most recognize.

When most evangelicals talk about a culture war they refer primarily to personal ethics, especially those issues that have become or are becoming normalized—like premarital sex, divorce, alcohol and drug use, pornography, and of course abortion and homosexuality. Issues like adultery, domestic abuse, cheating in school or business are also areas in which the surrounding culture rubs off on us Christians, but no one is trying to defend those behaviors, so the "culture war" talk doesn't usually include those. There are also other areas where lifestyles inside and outside the church are hardly distinguishable from each other on issues like materialism, consumerism, and consumption. But those areas *really* get little mention. They shouldn't be so overlooked.

While I don't dispute the importance of personal and sexual morality, this was hardly the focus of Jesus' ministry and certainly wasn't the reason for his debates with the Pharisees. They too were calling people to a higher moral standard. They criticized Jesus for associating with people with low moral standards. They challenged Jesus to uphold the Law's requirements when they brought a woman to him caught in the act of adultery. Jesus wouldn't condemn her although the Law required death.

Jesus issue with the Pharisees was their concern for religious rules coupled with a lack of concern for people. He told the Pharisees, "You [even] give a tenth of your spices—mint, dill, and cumin. But you have neglected the more important matters of the law—justice, mercy, and faithfulness" (Matt. 23:23). What justice and mercy issue was Jesus referring to? Just before that in verse 14 Jesus says, of Pharisees, "You hypocrites! You [foreclose on] widows' houses and for a show make lengthy prayers" (also Luke 20:47). Jesus is calling for a deeper break with the surrounding culture than our sexual morals. He is calling for different business and economic practices. He says, "Where your treasure is, there will your heart be also" (Matt. 6:21). Today we simply say, "Follow the money." Jesus clearly expects that following him will change our financial priorities, and that this change will go well beyond our tithing to the deeper issues of economic justice and mercy.

In the next chapter I will say more about the issue of money, but here is a quick rundown of what Jesus had to say on the subject. He spoke about not "storing up treasure on earth," and "It is easier for a camel to go through the eye of a needle, than for someone who is rich to enter the kingdom of God," and "You cannot serve both God and money," and "Woe to you who are rich," and "Sell your possessions and give to the poor," and the poor widow who gave her last penny, and the "worries of this life and the deceitfulness of wealth," and the fool who says, "I will tear down my barns and build bigger ones." Then, as I already noted earlier, there is the story of the rich man who ignores poor Lazarus right under his nose and goes to hell for it, and a judgment scene where the "saved" and the "un-saved" are separated like a shepherd separates the sheep from the goats based on our response to those in need all around us (Matt. 6:19, Mark 10:25, Matt. 6:24, Luke 6:24—and James 5:1, Luke 12:33, Mark 12:41-44, Mark 4:19, Luke 12:18, Luke 16:19-31, Matt. 25:31-46).

That's just ten passages about money and the poor and Jesus had even more to say on the subject. We could go on to mention hundreds of things that 1 John, the book of James, the Prophets, and the Law had to say about hanging onto our wealth in the face of the poverty all around us. Jim Wallis often makes the point that the Bible has over 2,000 verses about wealth and poverty. Yet much of the church says so little about this major emphasis of the Bible.

I find that Christians and missionaries who are from countries in Africa, or Asia, or Latin America often see much more clearly from the perspective of those countries the huge problem that wealth is in the American church.

When the church isn't calling people to live differently than the surrounding culture in such an important public area of their lives, perhaps we shouldn't be surprised that they mirror the culture in the more private areas as well. Most people would agree, even if they make excuse for themselves, that they *shouldn't* be involved in adultery, or divorce, or abuse of all kinds. The church teaches against those things, but people just fall short.

Most of the church, however, isn't even calling people to look at their luxury cars, their second homes, their designer clothes. Churches may do money management classes and

talk about tithing, but it's often in the context of helping people to be more financially successful. Those who are financially successful, however, are left alone if they are giving
generously to the church. They usually aren't being challenged to live financial lifestyles any different than those of
non-Christians. Jesus says, "Where your money is your heart
will be there also."

Like the Pharisees, are we more concerned about
morals—"Christian values"—and public prayers? Or about
sharing our wealth with the poor as Jesus and all the
prophets call us to do? If Christians are so concerned about
not giving in to the surrounding culture, why aren't we
standing in opposition to the prevailing culture on social and
economic issues?

Shouldn't Christians feel uncomfortable when our political, and economic, and social policy positions essentially
mirror the politics, economics, and social policy of the most
wealthy and most powerful people in the most wealthy and
most powerful nation in history? Do we think money and
power don't corrupt like they used to? Was Jesus talking
about something else when he said you cannot serve both
God and money?

Since we all tend to look out for our own selfish interests,
the church should be more discerning regarding the self-jus-
tifications (and propaganda) of those who hold power and
wealth. Jesus' clash with the religious and establishment
leaders of his day should give us second thoughts about too
closely aligning with wealth and power today.

Do our social and economic policies reflect God's concerns? Does anyone really believe that God's priorities are to
cut what we spend on the poor and elderly? Can anyone
think God is concerned that too many immigrants are getting into our country? Or that the wealthy are being taxed too
heavily? How does our Christian faith distinguish us from
non-Christians in these areas?

There is another still more public and corporate area
where the evangelical church is also not teaching a different
ethic or approach than what non-Christians hold: militarism.
In Chapter 7 I will say more about this, but I want to touch

here on how it relates to our being swallowed up in our culture. Although traditionally the church has tried to influence war policies by talking about "just war" criteria, the effect on actually curbing war has been virtually nonexistent.

Never in history can I recall the church saying no to a war the nation's leaders wanted to fight. Individuals within the church or a handful of small denominations have opposed certain wars or all wars. Some church leaders including the pope, did speak out against the wars in Iraq, but Catholic soldiers in the military paid no attention, went right ahead, and remained in good standing in their churches. Bottom line—there is no discernible difference between the military policy positions of most Christians and non-Christians.

Jesus had so much to say about the least being greatest, about taking up our cross and not a sword, about loving enemies (and he meant the Romans who occupied Israel). Surely Jesus should have some influence even on churches that believe sometimes war is necessary. Otherwise what distinguishes them from non-Christians? We need to be much less enamored of violence and fighting as a way to settle national differences.

I believe that when we sell out so completely to the surrounding culture in the areas of consumerism, materialism, and militarism, we shouldn't be surprised that the rest of our personal life follows. When the church does not address areas in which we so utterly fail to reflect the Jesus we claim as Lord in our corporate lives, we will reap a church that disregards Christ in our private lives as well.

Perhaps church members take their cues from the church's position. When the church teaches that in the "real" world (as the world defines reality) of sinful, fallen people and nations, we can't literally follow the teachings of Christ and survive, maybe we sabotage Jesus' message of a higher reality and a higher priority. If we as church leaders actually believed and taught Jesus' words about taking up our own cross and losing our life to gain it—if we laid our own lives on the line to follow Jesus, maybe others would follow. Then maybe the personal lives of church members would reflect a real commitment to Jesus as well.

ARE WE PASSING THE "SMELL TEST?"

Paul says, "For we are to God the pleasing aroma of Christ among those who are being saved and those who are perishing" (2 Cor. 2:15). So do we smell like Jesus? Or do we smell more like our surrounding culture? There are gospel preachers today who offer a message of intolerance and hate rather than reconciliation. Paul warns the Corinthians about false teachers masquerading as servants of righteousness (2 Cor. 11:13-15). We need to beware of such leaders, but I believe most Christians fall into a much more subtle accommodation with their culture.

Many pastors and church leaders are sincere Christians from Bible-believing churches who intend to follow Jesus, but somehow they miss the heart of Jesus. They believe in the virgin birth and the death and resurrection. They might even wear WWJD (What would Jesus do?) bracelets. They just don't think much of the stuff Jesus taught actually applies to their real lives.

The three hot-button issues everyone says to avoid—politics, money, and sex—are all things Jesus addressed. The church talks about sex but doesn't sound much like Jesus who was a friend to the prostitutes and sinners who mostly stay as far from church as they can. The church almost entirely ignores most of the things Jesus had to say about money. And all Jesus' words about loving enemies with a despised occupying Roman army as a constant backdrop have been largely taken out of the political context in which they were spoken and made irrelevant to our own economic, political, and military situations.

So throughout history the church ended up with lots of Christians whose lives utterly failed to reflect the Jesus they claimed as Lord of their life. Christians have been involved in terrible and evil things that were so much a part of their culture they didn't even give a thought to the vast chasm between their lives and the Jesus of the Bible they claimed to believe as the very Word of God.

There are many historical examples of this—slave-owners in the U.S. South thought of themselves as sincere Christians while they were buying and selling other people. A few generations later churchgoing men participated in lynching black men and thought of themselves as upholding the law and protecting their women and their community standards. Christians in Germany fought for Nazi Germany and thought they were just being patriotic and obeying the government. We can look back on all those and wonder how in the world they could have been so blind to the evil.

How do you think most Christians in Germany went along so easily with the Nazis? How could Christian folks in the South proudly pose for a photo op with their families in their Sunday best next to the latest black man they lynched? A few years ago James Allen and John Littlefield published *Without Sanctuary*, an entire book of lynching pictures, many on postcards. Look it up on Google. It is chilling.

In 2007 a friend of mine worked on a construction crew with other men who all considered themselves Christians—most attend church. Their attitude about the Iraq war was that we should just go over there and "bomb them all!" Gone was any nuance of liberating the Iraqis or creating a democracy or freeing them from the terrorists—just "bomb them all." I know, I know, this wasn't a very thought-out response and didn't represent the thinking of most conservative Christian leaders and thinkers. Still, how could it even show up among church-going folk? At some gut level an awful lot of Christians respond favorably to a "kick-butt" mentality. Are they listening to Jesus at all?

How can *anybody* think we can want to just kill them all and still be Christian? Is it because leaders and thinkers and preachers have separated questions about war from having anything to do with being a Christian or being saved. Have they made it a political question which shouldn't be the concern of the church? Is that how German Christians went along so willingly with the Nazis?

In fact in conservative churches from the pew to the pulpit to the famous personalities, the followers of the "Prince of Peace" are some of the strongest supporters of the military in the United States. I don't just mean they support military people. They strongly support military solutions to our country's conflicts. I think it's fair to say that conservative

Christians generally are *more* supportive of war than their secular counterparts.

When the church fails to make the connection between following Jesus and the real lives and issues of real people, then people will just fill in their own ethic—or rather the world's ethic along with the world's brokenness. It isn't that they don't intend to follow Jesus. It's just that they don't think of their current crises as having any real connection to their religious faith or to being a Christian, because much of the church isn't making the connection either.

PRAGMATISM OR PARANOIA?

When the church does make a connection between political events and its faith, the church has often made the wrong connection, opting for hard-nosed realism over Jesus' "idealism." It was hard-nosed realists who killed Jesus. Pilate and the leaders of the Sanhedrin were all hard-nosed realists. Pilate couldn't allow a threat to the peace or to his authority. Caiaphas the high priest was just being pragmatic and practical about the threat Jesus posed. He said if they let Jesus keep on doing miracles like he was doing, everyone would follow him, and then the Romans would step in and they would lose both their temple and their worship and then their whole nation. He added that it would be better for one man to die than to put the whole nation at risk of being destroyed (John 11: 47-50).

Bottom line: Jesus was a threat to their way of life and their freedom of religion. So serious secular and religious leaders joined forces to have Jesus killed for the "good of the nation."

Hard-nosed realists continue to raise the threat levels to mobilize people against whatever threatens their power. The threat warnings are always defined as being in the people's interest (even when they aren't). We get sucked so easily into the latest fear or hatred. I still remember an evangelist in my community during the 1950s preaching about the communist threat. The godless communists were about to take over our country. He predicted that unless there was a sweeping religious revival in our nation, or unless the Lord returned, that the communists would take over our nation within ten years. I was around eleven or twelve years old, and I was very scared.

In the early 1960s there was a billboard in our little central Illinois town that claimed Martin Luther King Jr. was a communist. In that one billboard was displayed two misplaced and exaggerated fears—our fear of civil rights for people of color and our fear of communism. I didn't know of any local Christians who protested either fear. Now few believe the communists were even close to taking over our government. And nearly everyone thinks Martin Luther King was a hero.

Today the threat is either from terrorists. Or more generally Muslims. Or all the undocumented immigrants in our nation. Once again many Christians are just as fearful and vocal and paranoid as any of the non-Christians. Their faith isn't helping them think any differently than the people with no faith. A lot of the fear is really pretty silly.

I lived in San Antonio, Texas, for over fifteen years. There were many undocumented immigrants in that city of sixty-five percent Latinos. Some of them were my close friends. It wasn't a big political issue in San Antonio. Politicians didn't run on anti-immigrant platforms, editorials didn't rail against undocumented immigrants, and letters to the editor weren't full of the matter.

Then I visited northern Indiana where there is a growing Latino population, and it was a huge issue. Politicians were running their campaigns on immigration concerns, editorials were full of the "immigrant problem," and many of the letters in the paper were about all the problems these Mexicans were causing. You would have thought immigrants were taking over the community, which was pretty funny since San Antonio didn't find a much larger population of undocumented workers to be a big deal at all. In fact San Antonio knew that if the undocumented workers were all sent back, the city would fall apart.

I think immigration has become such a concern in some settings because people in close-knit communities are suspicious of people who are different or outsiders and because a few TV and radio personalities and politicians have made this their soapbox issue. If you rant about something long enough you can stir up people's fears and paranoia and make them feel truly threatened. We get sucked into the culture's anxieties even quicker than into its "morals."

Essentially that is what happened in Germany. For centuries Jews were hated and mistrusted. Nearly everyone, including Christian opponents of Nazism, still believed Germany had a serious "Jewish problem" that needed to be addressed. Even Karl Barth, the famous German theologian who opposed the Nazis and became a defender of the Jews for theological reasons, preached an Advent sermon in 1933 in which he denounced Jews as "an obstinate and evil people" (*Hitler's Willing Executioners*, by Daniel Jonah Goldhagen, p. 113).

So when the Nazis came along with a "solution," most Germans, feeling *something* needed to be done, allowed first the confiscating of Jewish property, then the rounding up of Jews and then their deportation to God knew what fate. Christians to a large extent went along and participated in this along with everyone else. Christians should be sobered by our ability to be taken in by the evil and hate around us.

Today there is a lot of talk in both political and religious circles of Islamo-facists and terrorists. Most politicians are careful to distinguish between thousands of law-abiding Muslims in this country and a much smaller group of radicals who have hijacked the Muslim faith to fight a war of terror against the West. But other religious and political leaders and political pundits are painting the entire Islamic faith as essentially evil. They are trying to awaken America to this evil threat. They paint Allah as some strange deity worshipped by Muslims.

This is a total misunderstanding of the Arabic language. Christian Bibles used by Arabic Christians throughout the world also use the name *Allah* in reference to God. Allah is the Arabic word for God. Muslim Arabs trace their roots back to Abraham through Ishmael the son of Hagar, Sarah's servant who bore Abraham his first son. In the Bible God promised both Abraham and Hagar that he would make of Ishmael a great nation.

Muslims are adamant about there being only one God. Jews, Christians, and Muslims all trace their roots back to Abraham, and all share his belief in the one and only God. Christian missionaries working among Muslims would find it much more difficult to evangelize Muslims if they tried to start from the point of convincing Muslims that their God is a false God and they must accept a different God. Instead many follow Paul's example on Mars Hill in Athens. Paul saw an altar to the "unknown God" and proceeded to explain Christ as that "unknown god."

Missionaries to Muslims declare Christ as the fullest expression of the God that Muslims already love and worship. Muslims already believe in Jesus as a great prophet. The Koran speaks of Jesus, but like the Jews, Muslims don't accept Jesus as divine or believe in his resurrection.

The Koran does include difficult parts, but then so does the Old Testament Law, which prescribes stoning for many infractions of the law. Like most Christians, many Muslims do not believe those passages should be applied today. Declaring the Muslim faith as evil does little to build bridges of reconciliation and understanding, and it demonizes a whole people. It certainly makes sharing the gospel with Muslims far more difficult. How can we be messengers of reconciliation, as Christians are called to be, if we are filled with judgment and even hatred for the Muslim faith?

I am afraid for our country that if we experienced new waves of terrorist attacks there could be a popular cry for much greater repression of all Arabic or Muslim people fueled by this kind of intolerant speech. We did it in the past and could do it again.

In our free country we confiscated businesses and rounded up all Japanese citizens and non-citizens alike and put them in detention camps during World War II. We didn't exterminate them like the Nazis, but we still wonder why we treated Japanese-American citizens like we did. We are always horrified at what we allowed, but the horror comes *after the fact*.

Maybe we should be looking *now* with God's eyes at all those we fear so much and are hateful toward. Instead of being ready to break up families and round up and deport millions of undocumented immigrants who work hard and often pay taxes and own businesses in this country, maybe we should ask what Jesus would do. What did God say to Israel about how they should treat the aliens in their midst? We also were once aliens to this country. Many of our people were once hated as well.

WHERE DO WE LOOK FOR SOLUTIONS?

I do not suggest the immigration issue has simple solutions. The question of why immigration has exploded isn't simply a matter of people wanting American jobs. Why would so many people *literally* risk their lives to leave their home communities, often leaving family behind with the intent to send money back to them that they earn from minimum wage jobs?

Some suggest trade policies like NAFTA have destroyed the Mexican farm economy for several million farmers, leaving them with no way to earn a living. They can't compete with American grain raised with huge government subsidies and dumped into the Mexican market. So in desperation they come here so their families can live. What would you do? Watch your family starve while you got on a ten- or fifteen-year waiting list to immigrate legally?

Solutions to all the conflicting interests aren't easy, and I don't want to suggest that I have the answers, but I do know where we should be looking for answers. And I am sure that how we answer matters a great deal to Jesus. So as we look for solutions we should step back from our culture's mostly self-centered and fearful way of seeing and ask if the problem is really even a problem or just trumped-up paranoia masquerading as hard-nosed realism.

Then if there is a real issue, we should ask what the response of Christians and the church should be. How can we see with God's eyes? How will we care for the least of these? How can we bring about reconciliation and break down walls of hostility that divide us from one another? That is the calling of the church and is our mandate. Our ministry of reconciliation is the good news the church brings to a broken and often alienated world. It's as though Jesus was making his appeal to the whole world through us to be reconciled (2 Cor. 5:16-20).

In the New Testament church, reconciliation meant breaking down walls between Jews and Gentiles. Jews had no dealings with non-Jews if they could avoid it. The miracle of the early church is that Jews and Gentiles, who feared and hated each other broke free of their culture and became one family who worshipped and ate together like sisters and brothers in Christ. Who are the "Gentiles" today? Are we building up or tearing down the walls that separate us?

Chapter Four

BUT WE PERFORMED MIRACLES

Many will say to me on that day, "Lord, Lord, did we not prophesy in your name and in your name drive out demons and in your name perform many miracles?" Then I will tell them plainly, "I never knew you. Away from me, you evildoers!"
—Matthew 7:22-23

Don't you find Jesus disturbing? These sound like fine folk. They're prophesying in Jesus' name, even casting out demons and performing miracles in Jesus' name—but Jesus calls them evildoers! Who are these evildoers, anyway? Jesus doesn't spell out for us what is so bad about these people except to say, "By their fruits you will recognize them."

Maybe they are judgmental or unforgiving. Maybe they are prophesying and casting out demons to get rich. I suspect some TV preachers are just trying to get people's money, but Jesus says there will be "many"—lots of people who do miracle healing, and prophesy in the name of Jesus. This sounds like the kind of people we wouldn't think of criticizing—sincere Christian folks who go to church regularly, maybe more regularly than most of us.

Furthermore, I like these folks and usually feel right at home in their worship. I didn't grow up in a charismatic church, but whenever I'm around charismatic Christians I usually feel a real authentic heart-stirring faith. I think all of us long to experience the presence of God and to realize God at work in our lives. Around evangelicals in general I'm usually in agreement with the emphasis on being born anew and turning my life over to Jesus, repenting of my sins, and accepting God's forgiveness.

But I'm always suspicious that, despite all the good folks in most churches I've attended, something is missing. I suspect Jesus had something a little more earthshaking in mind than what passes for church for most of us. A friend of mine remarked about how at every service, in the rather fundamentalist church he often attended, he heard pretty much the same message—the plan of salvation and the danger of not accepting Jesus as your Savior. The assumption was that once you have made that all-important decision to accept Christ, you're in. You're saved. The problem for him wasn't so much what was preached and taught but what was left out.

Most churches probably have a somewhat broader range of sermons, but isn't that the focus of much of the evangelical church—that through the death and resurrection of Jesus we have been made right with God? We have forgiveness of sins. If we believe that, turn to Jesus, and repent of our sins we will be saved. Specifically we will be saved from hell when we die and will instead be eternally with the Lord. As Christians we are expected to live a renewed life. However, if we are already essentially upright moral people, our life will not be essentially different in detail, only in focus.

On the other hand, those who are essentially immoral, or drunks, drug addicts, cheats, swindlers—lawbreakers in any civilized society—have to turn from such ways and live as upright citizens. So in real life the message of repentance, as it generally plays out, calls for serious change among "bad" people. However, "good" people face only a recognition that their goodness is not nearly sufficient to deserve God's favor; only by also accepting Christ's death and resurrection as an atonement for their sin, right along with the "bad" people, can they enter into eternity with God. That is a crass way of stating it and maybe not fair. But that is pretty much how it works in most of the church. Isn't it?

Of course on top of this essential Christian message, there are many sermons and books and magazines that emphasize the many aspects and challenges of the Christian life like prayer, reading the Bible, sharing the good news, doing acts of charity, going to church, and just being loving, kind, generous, and all the other fruits of the Spirit. None of these affect the Christian's salvation, because we can't earn it, but they are certainly good additions since we are called to live new lives and because we claim Jesus as our Lord and Master.

The central message of Jesus, on the other hand, calls for repentance and a complete reordering of our lives *particularly* for good, upstanding, religious folks. Those were the very people Jesus really challenged. Actually he really got under their skin. The "bad" and disreputable folks flocked after Jesus and accepted his message of complete life makeovers. The "good" folks with most to lose in any real reordering stood on the fringes and criticized. They asked skeptical questions and were offended that Jesus didn't see their essential goodness. They resented his lax attitude toward the "bad" crowd who followed him.

If we actually take seriously what Jesus said, isn't he calling all of us to a complete reordering of our lives? Including and especially us good folks? His words of condemnation were almost entirely directed at the religious folks and not at the sinners.

JESUS' TEACHINGS WEREN'T OPTIONAL SUGGESTIONS

Jesus never suggests that belief in him is the essential aspect of salvation and following his teaching is an auxiliary option. Just before Jesus' words above about those protesting, "But we cast out demons," he says, "By their fruit you will recognize them. Not everyone who says to me, 'Lord, Lord,' will enter the kingdom of heaven, but only the one who *does* the will of my Father who is in heaven" (vs. 20-21).

He follows with, "Therefore everyone who hears these words of mine and *puts them into practice* is like a wise man who built his house on the rock. . . . But everyone who hears these words of mine and *does not put them into practice* is like a foolish man who built his house on sand" (vs. 24, 26, emph. added). This whole section of ten or fifteen verses at the end of Matthew 7 is Jesus' conclusion to his Sermon on the Mount and is therefore a warning to those who hear the sermon that they must now put it into practice in their lives. Jesus is clearly saying that to follow his teaching is to do God's will; only those who put his teaching into practice can enter into God's reign. These teachings, that seem to us upside-down, counter-intuitive, and against common sense Jesus says are the only solid ground on which to build our lives.

The shorter version of this sermon in Luke 6, the "sermon on the plain," ends with exactly the same admonition. But Jesus' teaching in these sermons is the very thing the church is uncomfortable accepting. In the church we hear a lot about Jesus' death and resurrection and salvation but little about how Jesus actually taught us to live in this sermon that stretches across three whole chapters in Matthew and a chapter in Luke.

1 John 2:3-6 makes the same point:

> We know that we have come to know him if we keep his commands. Whoever says, "I know him," but does not do what he commands is a liar, and the truth is not in that person. But if anyone obeys his word, love for God is truly made complete in them. This is how we know we are in him: Whoever claims to live in him must live as Jesus did.

WHAT ARE WE MISSING?

Sermons are a good gauge of what pastors think is important. If Christians fail to *follow* Jesus' teaching it may just be a sign of their sinfulness and imperfection for which they need God's grace and forgiveness. If pastors fail to *preach* what Jesus taught it is a more deliberate choice of priorities— it shows what we are choosing to emphasize and what to downplay. So preachers think they are being bold by preach-

ing about hell and warning people of God's judgment if they
don't get their life in order. "Getting your life in order"
means primarily accepting Jesus as your personal Savior. Of
course nearly everyone in church has already done that—
maybe many times. What would take real courage would be
to start telling the congregation to follow what Jesus says
about money.

How often are pastors preaching against storing up
treasure on earth? How many sermons about the rich man
who ignores poor Lazarus right under his nose? Or any of
the ten passages I mentioned in the previous chapter in
which Jesus talks about money (Matt. 6:19-20, 13:22, 19:21,
25:31-46, Mark 10:25, 12:41-44, Luke 6:20-24, 12:16-21, 16:13-
15, and 16:19-31)? How much is said about loving our enemies and praying for those who persecute us and doing good
to those who hate us? How often are we called to take up our
cross and follow Jesus?

I can't tell you how many sermons I've heard, with the
message that having wealth isn't a bad thing in itself, it's just
our attitude toward it. But if someone is gathering or storing
up wealth, doesn't that pretty clearly demonstrate one's attitude toward wealth? If I collect antique furniture, it's because I love antiques. Jesus clearly made the wealthy uneasy
about their stored-up wealth, which is not what most
churches are doing. The church constantly downplays Jesus'
words against dangers of storing wealth.

That isn't to say Jesus spoke against honest business people. He and the prophets speak against those who take *advantage* of their workers or oppress and exploit them. There
are good and honest business people who provide employ-
ment for many others in their communities, who show a real
concern for their workers and for the community. Then there
are others who squeeze all the profit they can from their
workers, keep their wages as low as possible, or even move
their factories elsewhere to find workers who will work for
even less. All the while they enjoy a lavish lifestyle far beyond what any of their workers can afford. They show concern for their bottom line only. Across the entire Bible God
judges those who oppress the poor and don't pay their work-

ers a fair wage (Jer. 22:13, Amos 5:11, Mal. 3:5, James 5:4-6). Poor wages must really be a big deal to God.

In the book of Revelation, when the seven seals are opened, with each seal comes another great calamity—wars, plagues, religious persecution, and natural catastrophes. When the third seal is opened the calamity revealed is "a quart of wheat for a day's wages." That's either terribly meager wages or way overpriced wheat—one of the seven great evils that humanity has to endure (Rev. 6:5-6)!

Jesus warned repeatedly against hoarding the resources God has entrusted to each of us, while all around the needs of the poor cry out. Isn't that why he asked the rich young ruler with all his inherited wealth to give it all to the poor and then follow him? For the young ruler that was a deal breaker, because he couldn't give up his wealth. Jesus sadly watched him turn and leave, but let him go (Luke 18:18-25).

I heard a sermon about the rich young ruler in which the preacher explicitly said the problem wasn't his wealth but his *love* for money. Then the preacher asked what we loved too much—pornography, booze, gossip, sports? He ignored the central challenge of this story and never even suggested that money might be our downfall as well.

Are preachers afraid of making people uncomfortable with all their stuff and all the wealth they squirrel away? I imagine many of us running after the rich young ruler who turned sadly away from following Jesus to explain to him that Jesus didn't *actually* mean he needed to literally sell all his possessions and give his money to the poor. He just needed to change his attitude toward his money. He just needed to make Jesus his first priority, and as long as his money wasn't a big deal to him he could actually keep most of it as long as he gave generously to Jesus' ministry. Because, of course, how could Jesus continue his ministry without generous supporters like him?

When Jesus tells the story about the rich man who ignores poor Lazarus right on his doorstep, he even rubs in the point by saying the dogs had more pity and licked poor old Lazarus' sores. But after death the tables are turned; the rich man ends up in torment and poor Lazarus is in paradise with

Abraham. The rich man begs Lazarus to come have mercy on him; when that fails, asks him to at least warn his brothers, who are still living, to change their ways before it is too late (Luke 16:19-31).

Yet I've heard several sermons, twice at funerals, about the rich man and Lazarus in which the only point was that there is a hell. We need to be saved or can end up in hell like the rich man, as though Jesus told the story to assure us there is a hell. But Jesus' point is that the rich man ended up in torment precisely because he ignored poor Lazarus right under his nose. Jesus doesn't suggest that the rich man's problem was that he hadn't become "saved."

ECONOMICS AS A SPIRITUAL ISSUE

I don't think preachers are afraid so much as they just haven't thought of economics as a spiritual issue. Many Christian thinkers and writers and theologians actually minimize the importance of following Jesus' teaching. A significant number of Christians teach that the Sermon on the Mount, which includes much of Jesus' teaching about wealth, sets such a high standard it can only be followed in the coming kingdom of God when Christ reigns. That absolutely *cannot* be what Jesus meant, because we will not be persecuted for the sake of righteousness; we will not have enemies to love, or the poor to care for in the coming kingdom where God reigns. Jesus clearly meant his words to be lived out in this age.

Others teach that Jesus set the bar so high that no one could reach it, so we can only depend on the grace of God, since we all fall so far short. The problem with that interpretation is that Jesus simply gives no hint that he means it that way either. He keeps saying, "Unless you hear my words and *do* them." Jesus introduces a whole section of the sermon by saying that unless our righteousness exceeds that of the Pharisees, we certainly won't enter the reign of heaven. Then he follows that with a whole string of examples.

You have heard don't murder, I say don't hate. You have heard, don't commit adultery, I say don't look at another woman with lust. Don't divorce, don't swear an oath to enforce your words, don't retaliate but turn the other cheek. Jesus tells us to love our enemies and pray for those who persecute us, because God loves them and treats them equally. Don't do your giving to charity, or your praying, or your fasting to be noticed or to impress others. Don't worry about anything. Don't judge others, or you will be judged the same way. Don't store up treasure on earth.

One explanation I've read as to why Jesus couldn't have meant for us to take literally what he says about money is that this would just be a new pharisaical rule for us to follow, becoming just another kind of "works salvation." Dallas Willard in *The Divine Conspiracy* argues that people could just give their wealth to the poor and feel very self-righteous about themselves (pp. 108-116, also see Appendix 1). Furthermore, says Willard, we all know poor people who aren't at all godly; we also know people with lots of money who are sincere in their Christian faith. So Jesus couldn't have meant that money itself is the problem. He was simply trying to teach that neither having money nor being poor is a sign of God's favor or its lack.

While I agree with this last point, it doesn't explain why Jesus was so negative in what he said to the rich. In Luke 6:20-26, "Woe to you who are rich," is the counterpoint to, "Blessed are you who are poor." I can't help but believe Jesus actually thought money was a real problem that kept people from loving God and their neighbor.

When I reflect on all Jesus said about money, I don't think the problem is making money but rather if we make it at someone else's expense or how much of it we think we deserve to keep for ourselves. Money has a way of owning us. Money is power, and Jesus warns about the exercise of power (Matt. 20:25-28). In his letter to the Ephesians, Paul warns us about the "powers" we must wrestle against. Money, like sex, is not itself evil, but both money and sex can have a lot of power over our lives. In that sense they are powers we must wrestle against or they will control us.

The argument that giving our money to those in need might just become another form of "works salvation" could be applied to *any* good deed—tithing, providing hospitality, being kind to our mean neighbor, even witnessing about Jesus. We could become proud of any of those things to show what a good persons we are. We could count on any of those things to earn God's favor. That doesn't mean we shouldn't still do them. We could even be proud of our humility, but that hardly means we shouldn't still be a humble person.

The "works salvation" argument is a way of not having to wrestle with the challenge Jesus gave the young ruler. We could argue that any concrete action to apply Christian faith is just another kind of "works righteousness," but we would then end up with a faith that has no visible expression. James tells us that kind of faith is dead.

In other areas of life as well, we Christians often don't find Jesus very practical to follow. When he says we should give to anyone who asks and not expect it in return, we just can't believe he actually meant it. But Jesus was seeing how we so tightly grasp what we have, thinking that it is ours and we earned it.

Jesus on the other hand recognized that all we have belongs to God. This attitude goes all the way back to Deuteronomy 8:10-18, to God warning the Israelites that when they arrive in the Promised Land and

> build fine houses and settle down, and when your herds and flocks grow large, and your silver and gold increase and all you have is multiplied, then your heart will become proud and you will forget the Lord your God who brought you out of Egypt. . . . You may say to yourself, "My power and the strength of my hands have produced this wealth for me." But remember the Lord your God, for it is he who gives you the ability to produce wealth.

God is pretty clear about who gets the credit for our wealth. I heard someone say, "If you find a turtle on top of a fence post, you can be sure it didn't get there by itself!" In the same way people with wealth didn't get there without anyone else's help, and certainly not without God's grace. Nowhere in the Bible does God say to those with plenty,

"You worked hard for that and you earned it, so you deserve to keep it as long as you give a tithe." If all we have and all we are belongs to God, then the only question for us as stewards of God's possession is how God wants his possessions to be used.

It's easy to see how a lot of Christians have completely missed this attitude Jesus has about compassion and mercy and our own financial interests. So I can't be sure Jesus didn't really mean we should freely give our stuff to those who ask, since it's not ours in the first place. I know it flies in the face of our capitalist system, but quite frankly it doesn't look to me like Jesus was a capitalist at all. For Jesus it all belongs to God and the rule of compassion and mercy takes precedence over any economic theory and every law—religious or civil. I know that isn't common sense.

A friend of mine, on reading my manuscript, thinks I "underestimate the power of (let's call it) 'the world.'" He was referring to the seduction of consumerism. The pull of money and security are so strong he isn't sure we can overcome it on our own. Maybe we can only live in such a counter-culture way in the context of a supportive church community. Certainly in our own experience my wife and I were able to make decisions about living more simply because the churches we attended supported and preached the value of simple living and service. We felt other Christian brothers and sisters had our backs. We didn't need to keep up with the "Joneses" or live by "dog-eat-dog."

THAT'S ALL WELL AND GOOD BUT BUSINESS IS BUSINESS

When Jesus told his followers they couldn't enter the kingdom of heaven unless they were more righteous than the Pharisees, who made long prayers in the synagogue and then went out and foreclosed on widows' houses (Mark 12:39-40), maybe he was referring to an actual event. Maybe a poor widow (or widows) had lost her home and people were talking about it. I have no doubt that any Pharisee who might have done this to a widow foreclosed *legally* on her home. Jesus doesn't suggest it wasn't legal. He just said it wasn't right. Jesus based his morality on compassion and mercy, not the law.

I doubt the Pharisees thought what they were doing was wrong. They didn't feel ashamed or guilty. They might have felt sorry for the widow, but they still went ahead because they were completely justified. Business is business. You don't let your feelings get in the way.

A person I know well told me about a good Christian man who served in the church. He offered to take care of the finances of his sister-in-law whose husband died. She didn't know much about business. He was a very successful businessman. The widow and her former husband never had much. After she sold their home, her entire worth was about $60,000 plus her social security checks. So her brother-in-law told her he could put her money into a savings account at the bank, but if she would let him borrow the money for his own business, he would pay her the very same interest that she could get from the bank. So she agreed. That seemed fair enough to her. But what a deal for him! He got to borrow $60,000 at several percentage points below what he would have had to pay to borrow it from the bank, probably saving himself $1,500-$2,000 per year in interest.

He *could* have offered to pay her the same interest he would have paid if he had borrowed from the bank. That would have been considerably more than she could get from a savings account; then *she* would have gotten the good deal. But it would never have occurred to him to offer it. Just like it probably never occurred to him that he took advantage of a widow with less than a tenth of his wealth. Business is business, and the transaction had nothing to do with his Christian faith.

This same man read his Bible every morning at the breakfast table, he believed the Bible was God's word, and he believed in all such fundamentals of the Christian faith as salvation and grace and eternal life. He believed in all the doctrines and all the norms of personal piety. I'm sure he never took a drink. Those who knew him never heard him swear or tell a dirty joke. He didn't cheat on his wife and probably wouldn't have considered cheating on his taxes.

So how did he miss the wide and deep swath through the Bible from the Law through the Prophets and the Gospels and the epistles, especially of James and 1 John, about justice and mercy and compassion for the poor and the widows being a major concern of God? I think this is why: Although this man believed every word of the Bible was true, his understanding of Christianity and the Bible was based almost solely on salvation and belief in Jesus as his Savior. Justice and mercy and how you treat the poor weren't "fundamentals" of his salvation or faith, although they are at the heart of the biblical message from Genesis to Revelation.

In Jesus' parable the rich man begs Abraham to let Lazarus return from the dead to warn his brothers to not ignore the poor as he had done. Abraham tells him that his brothers have the Law and the Prophets who have already warned them to care for the poor. If they ignore the Law and the Prophets, they certainly won't pay attention to a poor beggar who returns to life either.

Maybe what is missing from the church's message is the practical ways our "salvation" works its way out in real lives and real situations. We tend to separate the mundane matters of economics from the spiritual matters of salvation. So it's easy to see how Christians can be preaching and even doing miracles in Jesus' name even as they are taking financial advantage of someone or ignoring the plight of the poor. I'm sure a lot of Christians would be more generous than the man who made money off his sister-in-law, but if the message of salvation doesn't include the financial implications, it's not Jesus' message.

Zacchaeus, the tax collector, got it. He said he would return four times the money to everyone he had cheated. Jesus' response was, *"Today salvation has come to this house"* (Luke 19, emph. added). Jesus and all the prophets clearly tell us that how we handle the economic issues is deeply connected to our salvation. Isn't that the repentance and complete reordering of our lives that Jesus calls us to—especially we who are good, upstanding, religious folks?

It doesn't matter a whit how strong your belief in the Scripture is if you miss or ignore one of its primary applications to your life. Besides the Bible's strong stand against idolatry—which includes the materialism and militarism of our culture—how you treat the poor is probably the predominant theme across the entire Bible. Whether you take advantage of the poor or just ignore their needs, God takes it as a personal affront. That is fundamental to the Bible's message in every age. God despises all our worship and praise (Amos 5:21, Isaiah 1:11-18) and confessions and sacraments and prophesying and miracles if we are ignoring the least of these. Jesus says *that* will be what is on "the final" (Matt. 25:31-46).

THE SECOND COMING

The end of the movie *Schindler's List* always makes me think of the second coming and judgment. Oskar Schindler, a German and a bit of a con man and a war profiteer during World War II, operates a factory in Poland during the war that uses concentration camp labor. Even his accountant is a Jew who keeps convincing Schindler to bring more and more of the Jews he knows to the factory. If they are working at war production their lives will be spared.

Schindler has to pay for each worker, but he keeps bringing in more and more workers whether he needs them or not. He cuts deeply into his own profits and finally into his own wealth to pay for more workers. He takes risks to his own safety to stand up to the Nazis to keep all his Jews.

When the war ends rather abruptly, and the Jews are all free to go, Schindler breaks down. Through tears he keeps saying, "I could have saved more." He thinks of things he could have pawned, money he could have used. His accountant assures him that the hundreds of lives he saved is enough. But Schindler is painfully aware of the fate of those he hasn't been able to save.

The second coming may be something like that. We go about our lives doing what seems so important while thousands starve. We are aware of their starvation and may even be doing a lot to help them, but at the end we will all realize we could have done so much more.

Are there political implications?

The good news is that there is a growing awareness among some evangelical Christians and churches that how we treat the poor is a deep concern to God. Conservative Christians, particularly young people, are adding concerns about poverty to their moral and political values. That is a very encouraging development. For too long Christian conservatives have seen the failures of some poverty programs and opposed nearly all government programs, including those proven to be effective. If they only opposed programs that aren't working and were putting forth better alternative programs, or were even *discussing* the problems of poverty, their criticism of current programs might have more integrity.

Some Christian conservatives claim the government shouldn't be in the business of helping the poor at all. The church should do that. The problem is that churches haven't begun to step up to the extent necessary to take up the slack if there were no government programs. I am aware of churches with programs that work intensively with a few families and individuals. Or they give some charity to a lot of people—food boxes, clothes, and help with some bills. If *every* church on every block was working intensively with a few families, that might go a long way toward addressing the problems of poverty. Until then, most churches actively involved in poverty ministries know that government must also play a major role.

Conservative criticisms of programs to help the poor usually assume poor people actually could work if they just would. In fact most of the poor I've worked with are poor because of serious illness, serious injuries, severe disabilities, serious mental illness. Many of the poor are too elderly to work. In those situations all the arguments that assume poverty is the fault of the poor fall apart.

There are thousands of people who were working hard, had good jobs with health benefits, and then got a serious illness like cancer. When they had to quit their job for health reasons, they lost their health insurance and ended up bankrupt.

I don't suggest that all of the many government programs to help the poor only serve those who can't help themselves. Nor have all of these programs been a great success. But the difficulty of addressing poverty and the problems in some programs hardly removes our responsibility to help those living in poverty. We need to find creative ways to aid the poor that do strengthen them, do give them incentives and empower them.

We have learned from experience that if we regularly give handouts to poor people who could be doing more for themselves, the poor are not strengthened. They become weakened and dependent. Conservatives use this as a reason to oppose any programs to aid the poor. I'm suspicious that a lot of the opposition to government poverty programs has a lot more to do with people wanting to keep their money than with any real concern for the poor.

I've worked with poor people long enough to understand the arguments about the effectiveness of various poverty programs. But how have we reached the point that some conservative Christians believe any national policy encompassing some responsibility of the well-off for the poor is immoral and even theft? The irony is that the share of our nation's wealth going to the wealthiest 1 percent or 10 percent just keeps growing while the rich cry about being robbed! They claim wealth is being transferred from the wealthy to those with less, yet amid exploding inequality, financial figures show the transfer of our nation's wealth has all been in the other direction for over forty years—away from the middle, working, and poorer classes and toward the wealthiest.

I believe poverty, here and abroad, is a national and not just an individual or church concern. Governments do collectively what we cannot accomplish as individuals, which of course includes tax and financial policies as well as assistance to those unable to take care of themselves. The Old Testament prophets not only prophesied against individuals who mistreated or ignored the poor, they also judged the nations who forgot the poor. Israel, as a nation, was warned again and again about God's judgment for ignoring or exploiting the widows and the fatherless.

If Christ is Lord over all kingdoms and rulers as we confess, doesn't it follow that, just as in our individual lives,
everything we have belongs to God, so too all the wealth of
the nations belong to God? As citizens of our nation, but also
as citizens of God's realm, shouldn't we be asking one question—How would God want our nation's resources to be
used? Would God call us to spend less on programs for the
poor and more for the military? What are God's priorities?

STRAINING OUT GNATS

Millard Fuller, founder of Habitat for Humanity, often
made the point that many people quote Jesus saying, "The
poor will always be with us," as something inevitable. But
Jesus is actually quoting from Deuteronomy 15:11, which
says, "There will always be poor people in the land. *Therefore*
I command you to be openhanded toward your fellow Israelites who are poor and needy in your land."

Jesus said the Pharisees tithed everything down to the
smallest details, even tithing their spices and herbs, but neglected the big stuff like justice and mercy and faithfulness.
He added that they would strain out a gnat but swallow a
camel (Matt. 23: 23-24). Does this sounds like those working
to get prayer into public schools while saying little about the
needs of those living in poverty or those with no healthcare?
Or those trying so hard to post the Ten Commandments in
public buildings while ignoring the Sermon on the Mount?
Which is more important either religiously or politically:
symbols of piety? Or real actions of compassion and mercy?

Tony Compolo makes the point by telling audiences that
thousands are starving every day while North Americans
have the lion's share of the world's wealth. Then he adds that
most of us don't give a "shit." Then he pauses. He notes that
his audience was probably far more shocked by the bad
word than the fact that thousands starved today. We worry
about the little stuff and ignore what is primary.

WHAT IS GOD'S WILL?

Ultimately I don't think God's concern is about the evil of money. It's about of our lack of compassion for those with little or nothing—our unwillingness to let go to help the poor. Years ago I heard John Perkins tell how young people would come to him and ask how they could know what God's will was for their life. He would begin to ask them what they wanted to be, how much they hoped to earn, where they wanted to live. Most of them already had answers to all those questions, so he felt they were really just trying to figure out how they could get God to fit into the life they had planned for themselves. He would tell them instead of asking, "What is God's will for my life?" try asking, "What is God's will?" Period.

In other words, what is God's will for the world? God's will is that "justice flow down like a mighty stream," that the hungry are fed, that the gospel is preached. We already know God's will from passages all over the Bible. Then the question for us is, How can I be a part of God's will? How can I be involved in what God wants for the world?

Such an understanding has reshaped my life. Most of my life I've worked in poor communities, providing better housing for people often living in shacks. Because I believe God's will is that people have a place to live that is safe, warm, and dry. That kind of work hasn't been very lucrative, but it certainly has had many rewards beyond money. I didn't set out to *not* make much money, but that's often what happens when you make choices based on criteria other than how well it pays. I have yet to find someone among the many I know who chose a life of service and regretted it.

SO WHERE IS THE GOOD NEWS IN ALL THIS?

For many of us things are sounding severe and austere. Isn't the Christian life supposed to be filled with joy? This seems more like a guilt trip. It sure doesn't sound like the good news of the gospel.

Look again at what Jesus actually says. He preaches about "Good news to *the poor*." He says in several different ways that one day the tables will be turned (Luke 6:20-26). "Blessed are you who are poor for yours is the kingdom of God." The counterpoint is "Woe to you who are rich, for you have already received your comfort." Might Jesus' message of good news to the poor actually *be* bad news for the rich? We *really* want to ignore such a sobering warning.

It is good news, however to those who like Paul can say, "I count everything as loss compared to the possession of the priceless privilege of knowing Christ . . . for his sake I've lost everything and consider it all to be mere rubbish in order that I may win Christ" (Phil. 3:8, *Amplified Bible*).

An unfortunate aspect of North American Christianity is that this theme of Jesus' teaching is not only overlooked in wealthy churches but in most poor churches as well. In poor churches too I've heard the story of the rich man and Lazarus preached solely as a warning about hell. Poor churches too often miss the point that God takes the side of Lazarus—that one day God will turn the tables. That one day the meek will inherit the earth and the wicked will be no more (Ps. 37:10-11). God condemns the powers that crush the powerless. To the downtrodden and hopeless, that is good news.

Most of the poor people I've known understand that God cares about them. They pray for a job, for money to pay the bills, for healing, for a miracle. "Give us this day our daily bread," is not an empty phrase. Unfortunately some are misled by the gospel of health and wealth. Misleading, because it creates fantasies of Cadillac's and diamonds and assures healing if only you have enough faith. Misleading because if the healing doesn't happen and the Cadillac doesn't materialize, faith is crushed. Misleading because it overlooks Jesus' real message that there is no need to worry if God looks after us. Real happiness is not in the abundance of things. And God has taken the side of the poor against all who ignore, oppress, exploit them.

All of us, rich and poor alike, are easily sucked into the American dream of always wanting more and the belief that God *wants* us to have more. Paul's assertion that he can do all things through Christ who strengthens him is often distorted as a triumphalist claim of power to overcome every obstacle.

Paul actually says he has learned contentment in any situation: "Whether well fed or hungry, whether living in plenty or in want. I can do all this through him who gives me strength" (Phil. 4:11-13).

I have seen this demonstrated best in the lives of some of the poor folks I've known. I repaired the leaky roof of an elderly lady who was in poor health. Her home was very run down but clean and well kept inside. Every time I went to work on her house she was smiling. Whenever I asked her how she was doing, her response, despite her circumstances, was always the same: "I'm blessed. I'm blessed." That is good news indeed.

Chapter Five

FUNDAMENTALISM THAT ISN'T SO FUNDAMENTAL

I'm not a fundamentalist. I guess I used to be one, but my study of history and especially church history gave me a broader perspective. I just couldn't sustain a fundamentalist approach even though I am still quite committed to following Jesus and taking the Bible seriously. If you just believe what you have always been taught, it doesn't take much thought or even much faith to just keep claiming the same things. But what if you come to the place you simply can no longer believe some of those things? My reading of science has raised some questions for me, but I'm not convinced that scientific dogma has all the answers anymore than religious dogma has.

However, my study of Scripture, the church, and the history of the Bible itself convinced me that the "fundamentals" of fundamentalism aren't actually that fundamental to the historic or biblical Christian church. I saw much of the fundamentalist church ending up farther from taking Jesus seriously than should be the case when claiming to take the Bible literally.

I was listening to a Christian call-in talk show while driving. They were discussing capital punishment, and a caller said he favored capital punishment because, after all, the

Bible says, "An eye for an eye." The Christian host agreed
and never said a word to note that Jesus had called his followers to a different response. I noted the ease with which a
Christian radio program that would have strongly defended
inerrancy of Scripture so smoothly sidelined what Jesus
taught.

Taking the Bible literally doesn't *have* to minimize what
Jesus said, if Christians also take Jesus literally. But so often I
see people soften or even cancel out what Jesus said that I
wonder if the way they read the Bible is actually part of the
problem.

So I write this chapter about fundamentalism not to start
a theological argument but to suggest that treating Scriptures as all equally authoritative weakens the *central* revelation of the Bible and isn't necessary to a historic understanding of inspiration. For me the Bible is the story of God's revelation of himself to humankind culminating in Jesus—God's
final Word, not just written on the page, but lived out in a
human life. Christians are not called to worship the Bible but
the One to whom it points.

The logic of fundamentalism is that every word of the
Bible is dictated (breathed) by God and must therefore be
true, and historically and scientifically accurate in every re-
spect—or else the whole Bible is called into question. If we
can question or judge any part of the Bible as being in error,
then we place ourselves over the Scripture. In essence, we
put our word above God's word. This is, however, a false
choice. We don't need to either accept every word as inerrant—containing no errors—or make every word subject
to our own reasoning if we recognize Jesus the Living Word
as God's fullest revelation.

The core of fundamentalism is a view of Scripture that is
itself neither fundamental to Christian faith nor to the
church's historic understanding of Scripture. Fundamentalists appear to take the Scripture very seriously, but they are
often so woodenly literalist that in the process of quoting
Scripture to bolster a point, like the radio talk show I mentioned, they end up canceling out or hiding the central truths
Jesus taught.

Jesus certainly didn't seem to have or teach a fundamentalist view of Scripture. Compassion for the needs of people always took precedence over scriptural laws about the Sabbath or purity rituals. He cancels out "An eye for an eye," (Exod. 21:23-25) with his own standard of turn the other cheek (Matt. 5:38-39). He keeps underscoring "But I say . . . " to recapture God's intent from the beginning. He always reinterprets or restates the Law to align it with what he sees as the basis of the Law: to love the Lord with all your heart and your neighbor as yourself.

The early church also did not view Scripture in a fundamentalist way. Paul clearly believed Christ superseded the Law so that the Law no longer applies to non-Jews. Yet he writes to Timothy that those same Scriptures (because there was no Scripture other than the Old Testament at the time Paul wrote his letters) are inspired by God. More literally he says they are "God-breathed." Despite his contention that we are now free from the law, Paul still says the Scriptures are useful for doctrine and correction and instruction in living a righteous life (2 Tim. 3:16).

Paul doesn't claim Scripture is useful for understanding science or history because our modern scientific and historical questions weren't being asked when it was written. Scripture wasn't written to answer all of our modern historical or scientific questions. To claim that the Scriptures are without error in every historic and scientific statement is more weight than the Scriptures need to carry—even though they are a reliable and inspired guide for living and for coming to faith in Jesus. The Bible itself doesn't claim to be without error. Fundamentalists have simply extrapolated scientific and historic inerrancy from the term *God-breathed*.

John 20:30-31 says Jesus did many other things, but *these things* are written to inspire belief that Jesus is the Messiah, the son of the living God. John's gospel was written to instill faith in God and in Jesus as Messiah and Lord. It wasn't written to provide a complete or even unbiased history of the events in Jesus' life. John had an agenda to instill belief.

Throughout most of the history of the church, the church has understood the New Testament as taking precedence

over the Old wherever the testaments differ in their depic-
tion of God or God's will for God's people. The New Testament has the greater authority. Fundamentalism sees every
word of both Testaments as being equally from the mouth of
God. So if God says, "an eye for an eye" or calls for the stoning of a disobedient son or demands the slaying of whole
tribes—men, women, and children—then that was his will
in the Old Testament. In the New, God is revealed to be dealing with humanity in a different way—through love and
grace.

But why would God change so dramatically? God is unchanging. Hasn't God's will for humanity always been the
way of love and reconciliation? We can see God's will perfectly revealed in Jesus, God's perfect Word—The Word not
written with human hands but expressed in Jesus' life. The
Word against which everything that precedes or comes after
is weighed and understood. As we saw earlier, Jesus understood all the Law and the Prophets to hang on the double
principle of loving God with all your heart and your neighbor as yourself.

When we look for it, we can see in the Old Testament examples of this God of love and grace and compassion—a
God who wants to bless all people of the earth. But Israel,
like much of the Christian church, "saw through a glass
darkly," and often mistook zeal for the Law or for ethnic purity as the will of God. If God's law forbade adultery, then
adulterers should be killed. If idolatry was evil, then it followed that people who worshipped idols were evil and
must be removed from their community.

Sometimes this meant having nothing to do with such
people; other times, don't marry them—or even put away
wives you have already married (as Ezra called for). Other
times this meant utterly wiping out such people. Such
killing devolved at times to ethnic cleansing of all non-Jews.
Anyone outside the community had to go.

This is a long way from the God revealed to us in Jesus
who spoke words of grace to outsiders. He spoke well of the
Gentile widow who fed Elijah and the Gentile Naaman
whom Elisha healed of leprosy. His words of grace toward

outsiders so infuriated his audience that they were ready to throw him off a cliff (Luke 4:20-30)!

WAS GOD DIFFERENT IN THE OLD AND NEW TESTAMENT?

There are two ways of resolving these differences between how God is portrayed. One is to say, as has been historically done through much of the church's history, that the New Testament is simply a more complete or fuller revelation of God. Jesus says if we have seen him, we have seen what God is like (John 14:9). If the revelation of the Old Testament had been perfect we wouldn't have needed the New to complete God's revelation to us. Hebrews 10:1 says that the Law was only a shadow of what was to come. What came was the perfection of Jesus Christ.

Fundamentalists resolve the differences between the Old and New Testament another way. They say both testaments are without error and both are the very words of God—therefore *God* changed, or at least God's requirements and laws changed, since both claim to give the very commands of God. Both of the testaments or covenants were perfect and without error in what God wanted for that time or dispensation. You only need to carefully read the details of the law in Exodus, Leviticus, and Deuteronomy to wonder if that is true (Deut. 22:28-29). Many Christians denounce Muslim Sharia law. Sections of the Torah sound just as horrific.

Many Christians might not spell out that God changed the rules in different "dispensations," to explain the differences between the God revealed in violent passages of the Old Testament and the God revealed in Jesus. They just assume that God commanded both annihilation of enemies and love for enemies, at different times and in different situations. But that so strongly colors and limits the words of Jesus that they cease to have much power or relevance, because we're left to decide in the heat of the moment which word from the Lord applies to our situation.

Western culture has renounced polygamy, so most Christians would never use the Old Testament to support polygamy today. But Western culture has not renounced war, so Christians frequently use Old Testament examples of war to justify it today. Until 150 years ago, a significant number of Christians used Old and New Testament precedents to support slavery. Now no one does. The point is, without a reference point like Jesus, all kinds of things can be justified with a passage from somewhere in the Bible.

HOW DID JESUS USE SCRIPTURE?

Jesus gives us a glimpse of how he viewed the scriptural laws when he said, "You have heard that it was said to the people long ago, 'You shall not murder, and anyone who murders will be subject to judgment.' But I tell you that anyone who is angry with a brother or sister will be subject to judgment." Then he corrects or adds to the Law with several more examples (Matt. 5:21-48). Thus in his own words Jesus supersedes the commands of the Old Testament Law.

These examples don't quite resolve, however, if Jesus is saying that God's rules changed or the Law itself was imperfect. But Jesus gives us a clue in what he says about divorce. He says Moses allowed divorce under certain conditions "because your hearts were hard" yet adds that this was not God's intention from the beginning" (Matt. 19: 3-9). Jesus goes back before the Law to the creation story itself and sees there what God's original intent for marriage was before we messed up. So the Law didn't reflect God's perfect will but was an accommodation to fallen people.

Isn't it true that each time Jesus says, "You have heard, but I say . . . " he is going behind the accommodation for a fallen people to reflect God's original perfect intent? In short Jesus sees the Law as less than God's perfect will.

What then does Jesus mean when he says,

> Do not think I have come to abolish the Law or the Prophets; I have not come to abolish them but to fulfill them . . . until heaven and earth disappear, not the smallest letter, not the least stroke of a pen, will by any means disappear from the Law until everything is accomplished. (Matt. 5: 17-18)

Indeed Jesus does bring to fulfillment or completion what in the Old Testament was unfulfilled and incomplete. However, he could hardly be saying all the Law as written must be followed, or he wouldn't have been able to say of the adulterous woman, "Let the person who is without sin cast the first stone" and follow that by telling the woman that he won't condemn her either and that she should go and stop sinning. The Law was clear; it said she should be stoned. The Pharisees made the Law more important than people. Jesus didn't argue about what the Law said; he simply applied the Law back on her accusers and showed compassion and forgiveness for her.

If Jesus had meant the Law stands as written, he wouldn't have said what he did about the Law on divorce and wouldn't have been as lax about purity laws—handwashing and who one can touch. Peter's vision of the sheet of unclean animals and his subsequent acceptance of Gentiles as brothers and sisters clearly contradicts the Law's requirements for clean and unclean. Paul's dismissing of the requirements of the Law regarding food offered to idols and circumcision for Gentile believers is also a clear indication that the early church didn't understand Jesus to mean that the Law was still the full authority it had earlier been in the lives of believers.

In whatever way we understand Jesus when he said "not one jot or tittle" shall pass away (KJV), we have to contend with all the ways Jesus, and the early church, assumed the Law was superseded in him. Certainly the early church and the historic Christian faith elevated the authority of Jesus above the Law and the Prophets of the Old Testament.

BINDING AND LOOSING

Jesus gave to the church the authority of binding or loosing. Scholars today understand this to refer to the method of the rabbis in interpreting Scripture. Where the Law might say that no one is to work on the Sabbath, it doesn't clarify what is and is not work. We are not to steal, but if I find a dollar in the parking lot is it stealing if I keep it? What about if I find a wallet? The rabbi might say it is not stealing to keep a dollar, in which case I am *loosed* from the Law. But I am *bound* by the Law if I find a wallet. A rabbi's interpretation was called his "yoke"—the burden he placed on his followers. This is what Jesus meant in saying his yoke was easy and his burden was light. (See Drury's "Who Says What the Bible Says? The Keys to the Kingdom, Binding and Loosing.")

Jesus gave to the church this authority to bind or loose—to determine how to apply Scripture and his teaching to our lives, "where two or three gather in my name" (Matt. 18:18-20). We do not decide individually but in communities accountable to each other and the Word. As followers of Christ we seek together to understand how Jesus intended for us to live out in our daily lives the things he taught. Just as Jesus puts new meaning into the Old Testament each time he says, "You have heard . . . but I say . . . " so he entrusts us to understand all of the Hebrew Scriptures in light of the risen Christ we follow. Jesus leaves us with the authority of making such interpretations and applications.

HOW HAS THE CHURCH VIEWED THE OLD VERSUS NEW TESTAMENT?

Historically, from its first several centuries, the church has seen the Bible as its book. Church leaders decided which books should be included in the Bible and therefore felt the church had authority over the Scriptures, since they had given the Scriptures their authority. This was the belief of the Christian church for 1500 years. Then with the Reformation, Luther declared that the authority of Scripture should be above the authority or traditions of the church, because Scripture reflected the earliest church with its living memory of the defining event of Christianity—Jesus' life, death, and resurrection. Therefore Scripture should be our only authority—*sola scriptura*.

But even Luther felt free to question the canon. He felt the book of James should not have been put into the Bible because of its emphasis on works. Luther felt the central message of the gospel was grace. He referred to James as an "epistle of straw." I would disagree with Luther on this point. To be honest, James sounds a lot more like the words of Jesus than Paul's letters. But the point is, even Luther who brought the church back to a reliance on Scripture alone didn't believe the whole New Testament was without error. Luther taught that the Scriptures were the "cradle of Christ." They are inspired *because* they bear Christ to us. Jesus himself is God's primary revelation.

Other reformers as well saw the New Testament as being more inspired or more authoritative than the Old, which was a less perfect revelation of God. If the Old Testament had been a perfect revelation we wouldn't have needed the Word revealed to us in Jesus and the New Covenant. Jesus suggests that God's will is unchanging, but the earlier Law does not always reflect God's perfect will. Jesus fulfills or brings to completion our understanding of God. Throughout the church's history, Scripture has been viewed as inspired by God, but the church has not historically referred to it as "inerrant."

To illustrate the difference, if you read a great book or hear a great sermon that may have been life-changing for you, you will say that sermon or that book was really inspired. You may say God really spoke to you through that preacher or that writer. That doesn't mean you believe they were inerrant. There may even be parts of what they said with which you disagree, but you still believe the sermon or book was inspired (though I am *not* suggesting that any book or sermon may meet the same standard of inspiration or authority as the Bible).

The Bible is our earliest record of Jesus' life and teaching and the life and teaching of the early Christian community that followed. The Bible has stood through millennia and has a historical and faith-tested weight that is not carried by any other writing or sermon. I see the Scripture as carrying far greater authority than any other writing.

I am simply making the point that defining something as inspired does not require us also to believe it to be "inerrant." In any event the real test of how much authority we give to Scripture is not the doctrine of inspiration we claim but the effect we allow it to have on our lives. What the Bible does in our lives is more important than what it is.

Fundamentalists usually think they are simply holding on to the "fundamentals" of the faith that have always been believed by the church. The primary way they do this is by their high view of Scripture and declaring it to be without error. By protecting or defending the Scripture against any question of its authenticity, its authority, its historical accuracy, or its authorship, they preserve what they think the church has always believed.

MODERNISM BROUGHT ABOUT FUNDAMENTALISM

In fact "Fundamentalism" is only a little over a century old and was a direct reaction to the rise of "Modernism." Modernist scholars began to look at the Bible rationally; through linguistic study they questioned if certain passages were additions and not part of the original. Because of writing style or words used, they questioned if a particular book was written when it said. Through archeological study and research into other civilizations in the Middle East, they questioned the historical accuracy of some of the Bible's stories, including the stories of Abraham, Isaac, and Jacob.

This has evolved to today's biblical minimalists who discount the historicity of any story that cannot be independently verified through other historical sources. Or take the Jesus Seminar scholars, who discount any stories of Jesus that seem miraculous or out of the ordinary—including the resurrection and virgin birth of Jesus. Through scientific study they question the scientific accuracy of certain stories and cast doubt on anything miraculous or supernatural.

Conservative scholars who began Fundamentalism as a movement defended the Bible from Modernism with a modern response. They declared that every word of Scripture was accurate and without any error in fact. The logic was that if *any* word of the Bible could be questioned or doubted, then *every* word was in doubt and was subject to the wisdom or whims of man. Therefore they declared every word was accurate even in every historical and scientific detail.

The problem is that the Bible wasn't written from a modernist perspective in the first place. The writers weren't answering modern scientific and historical but rather faith questions. They weren't primarily answering the "how" but the "why" questions. As historic movements, both Modernism *and* Fundamentalism were based on a fact-based way of looking at the Bible. Inheritors of either movement rely on modern understandings of wisdom which deal in facts and proofs. Both claim more than they should.

There is a lot of arrogance in thinking we can judge the accuracy of anything based on what we can prove from our own experience of the world as today's modernists do. There are also problems with claiming every word of Scripture is from God and without error when there are so many differing points of view within the Bible itself. I'll say more about this dialogue within the Bible in a later chapter.

It's not as though claiming every word of Scripture as inerrant and infallible will actually protect us from heresy. Many false cults and beliefs have arisen among those who claim they are following the exact words of Scripture. Nor does inerrantism assure a uniform set of beliefs among fundamentalists, who range across a wide array of denominations and groups, some of whom hardly even recognize each other as truly Christian.

There are other difficulties with claiming the Bible is without error. There are in fact discrepancies scholars have found between various passages. First Chronicles 21:1-8 says that Satan incited David to take a census of all his fighting men. Meanwhile 2 Samuel 24:1 says it was the Lord in his anger who incited him.

Matthew 27:3-8 and Acts 1:18-19 tell different stories about Judas' death. Both stories agree that there was a field near Jerusalem called the "field of blood" that had been bought with the thirty pieces of silver Judas received for betraying Jesus. Matthew says Judas returned the money to the temple leaders, threw it on the floor, then went and hung himself. The priests not wanting to return defiled money to the temple treasury used it to buy a field to bury foreigners. Acts says that Judas took the money and bought a field where he ended up falling headlong and his guts spilled out. There is no mention of suicide.

Each of the gospel writers has a slightly different remembrance of who went to the tomb on Easter morning. They agree that the women were the first witnesses but don't agree on which women were there. Matthew and Luke's birth stories are different. Both agree that Jesus was born in Bethlehem and grew up in Nazareth, but Matthew suggests Mary and Joseph lived in Bethlehem (Matt. 2:11) and moved to Nazareth after fleeing to Egypt, because they didn't trust Herod (Matt. 2:22-23). Luke says that following the days of purification, Joseph and Mary presented Jesus at the temple and then returned to their hometown, Nazareth in Galilee, with no mention of a trip to Egypt (Luke 2: 21-22, 39).

Considering that the Gospels were written probably fifty years after Jesus' death, we can expect that even eyewitnesses to these events would have had different memories, and the birth stories would have been *at least* second-hand accounts unless both Matthew and Luke interviewed Mary personally. We shouldn't be surprised at different memories. Authentic historical events are regularly remembered differently even by those who were there, especially fifty years later. But these differences *do* raise questions about the verbal inspiration that fundamentalists claim.

There are other examples of mistakes in numbers or succession of kings or historical events where one passage contradicts another. None of these examples are terribly significant. Even fundamentalist scholars acknowledge these discrepancies. Often they claim the errors were not in the original revelation or texts but were made over the centuries by various people who copied the books by hand.

The problem is that we no longer have a single original text of a single book of the Bible. All we have are copies of copies of copies with thousands of differences in wording, as noted by Bart Ehrman in his book, *Misquoting Jesus*. The author was at one time thoroughly fundamentalist and majored in the study of biblical texts and how they came to be in the Bible. His faith began based on a belief in the inerrant word of God. The problem he found was that there are thousands of variations in all the copies of ancient Hebrew and Greek texts we have and none of them are originals, so where were the inerrant words he had believed in? Today he is largely agnostic and has little faith in any religious tradition.

Some of his examples were significant and gave me a different perspective on those passages. Most of his examples, however, seemed insignificant and inconsequential. I couldn't see why he quit believing almost altogether. He claims his lack of belief stemmed from not being able to square a loving God with all the misery in the world. I can't help wondering if he based his faith on the wrong thing to begin with. His faith was in the Bible itself. This is one of the dangers of the fundamentalist mindset. When some of us begin to doubt the truth of one thing in the Bible, we can lose faith in everything, because that is the logic of fundamentalism.

I believe the biggest problem with fundamentalism is a belief in the Bible that for many overshadows belief in the words of Jesus. Stan Guthrie wrote an editorial in *Christianity Today* (October, 2007) questioning the validity of those claiming to be "red letter Christians"—those who give priority to the words of Jesus. He said in essence: So what's so special about the red letter parts of the Bible? It's all God's word. I was taken aback that a follower of Christ couldn't see any special significance that might give Jesus precedence over other parts of the Bible.

If every word of the Bible is from the mouth of God and without error, then Leviticus, and the letter to the Romans, and the words of Jesus are all equally the very words of God. So when Jesus says something, but in Leviticus God says something else, or the apostle Paul says still something else, then obviously Jesus didn't mean it the way it sounds. So Christians often come to an understanding of Jesus that fits with taking the Old Testament and the epistles as having equal standing. When they try to harmonize the contradictions between them, they end up canceling out or watering down the words of Jesus, who *should* be the touchstone for all of his followers.

The Old Testament *does* at many points reflect the God revealed to us in Christ. Jesus often quotes the prophet Isaiah. Some scholars suggest Jesus' understanding of his messianic role was drawn from or informed by his understanding of Isaiah's suffering servant. Amid experiencing God not as a set of rules to follow but as a close relationship lived in the Spirit, Jesus was deeply formed, as the Jew he was, by the Scriptures of his day. Through the close relationship Jesus had with his *Abba* Father he was also able to see a more complete and fuller picture of God in those Scriptures.

Jesus said that the old religious structures or doctrines couldn't be adapted to the new truth revealed in him. The new wine needed new wineskins (Matt. 9:16-17). The new, dynamic, moving, growing, fermenting movement of the Spirit couldn't be contained in the old legalistic ways of thinking. The Spirit can't be controlled or contained within the structures of rules and doctrines. You can't just sew this new patch into the old shirt. A life lived in the Spirit, which Jesus says will lead us into all truth (John 16:12-13), is far more dynamic than a set of rules or laws or proofs. We all have to continually examine our lives and our faith, our assumptions and our traditions, and ask the question—does this reflect the truth revealed to us in Jesus? Does my life reflect the Christ I claim as Lord?

In a new "postmodern" world perhaps we can see other approaches than the fundamentalist/modernist "actual facts" responses to scientific and historical criticism. The popular culture today is less enamored of science providing all the answers. Today many doubt the arrogance of modernism's assumptions that we can know or prove everything. We understand and accept that there are many things we cannot know. There are mysteries we cannot fathom.

Within this context, do we need to defend the Bible with proof of biblical facts, or the certainty of scientific knowledge? The real question in today's world is, Does the Bible make us a better people? A more compassionate people? Does it lead us to God? Those questions don't call for proof—but for story and poetry, dance and song. And isn't that closer to the context of the biblical writers anyway?

Chapter Six

CREATIONISM

For I resolved to know nothing while I was with you except Jesus Christ and him crucified.
—1 Corinthians 2:2

A friend of mine wants his geologist father to become a Christian. Once when he was telling me about his father he said, "Of course, since he's not a Christian, he believes the earth is millions of years old. We've talked about that," he said, "but we haven't really gotten anywhere with it because he's pretty convinced by the science."

I had this sinking feeling, not because my friend chose to believe what he thought the Bible said, but because his father, a scientist wouldn't be likely to consider a relationship with Jesus if he thought it included having to give up all he knew to be true from his life's work. What a shame to place a hurdle so non-essential to faith in Jesus.

Paul says he resolved to know nothing while he was with the Corinthians except Jesus Christ and him crucified. He admonishes Timothy to not waste time in foolish and stupid arguments (2 Tim. 2:23). Paul wants nothing to distract from the primary message of the gospel of Jesus. He wants nothing to discredit the message. He is willing for the cross in all its "foolishness" to be central (1 Cor. 1:18-25), but doesn't want any other foolishness getting in the way of

Jesus' good news of the kingdom. He really takes on the "Judaizers" for attaching Jewish rituals and law to the requirements of the gospel. He doesn't try to get Jewish believers to stop observing Jewish law themselves. He just doesn't think this should be required of non-Jews. As an unexamined article of a simple faith, a literal understanding of the creation story isn't a problem. As a dogmatic statement of inerrant doctrine necessary to Christian faith, it is harmful both to those receiving the message and to those conveying it. For someone growing up in the church, believing Genesis 1 may not be so much a real step of faith as just not having really thought critically about it. But some have given the creation story a great deal of thought and reflection and study. They have tried to use science to corroborate the story. Those efforts seem to me to be both bad theology and bad science.

I'm not suggesting that science has all the right answers. The shine has gone off of rationalism's promise to answer all of life's questions. Today's generation isn't so much looking for hard facts as for something to believe in and give meaning and purpose to life. So it's ironic that conservative Christians are raising the stakes so high at this time to promote creationism as a hard-fact alternative to science and even trying to get equal time in school science classes.

This whole issue of faith verses science is unnecessary and extraneous to the real claims of Jesus on our lives. I almost hesitate to take on this discussion. I don't think this question is going to be on "the final." After all, if some Christians want to believe that the Genesis 1 story of creation is scientifically and historically accurate, what's the harm? Why challenge their beliefs? I guess the answer is because many Christians raise the issue so vigorously and make it a litmus test of faith. According to them, if you don't believe Genesis 1 as literally factual, you don't believe in the Bible.

SCIENCE VERSUS FAITH—ACT I

Over five hundred years ago the church had another serious dispute with science. Scientists like Copernicus and

Galileo claimed that the earth was round. They became convinced that along with Venus, Mars, and Jupiter, the earth was a planet that revolved around the sun. The church believed this contradicted the clear teaching of Scripture. Psalms 104:5 says, "He set the earth on its foundations; it can never be moved" (see also Ps. 93:1, 96:10, 1 Chron. 16:30, and Eccl. 1:4-5). They demanded that Galileo recant his teaching or be declared a heretic. Galileo complied. Copernicus was more cautious in putting forward his theories and didn't publish his ideas until near his time of death. Even then the church repressed his ideas. Only recently did the Catholic Church formally acknowledge that both scientists were right.

At the time, Galileo and Copernicus were simply noting what they saw and trying to make sense of it. How the sun and moon and planets and stars revolved and moved across the sky only made sense if the earth and planets were orbiting the sun. They could only prove it with complicated mathematical and astronomical formulas. They didn't have satellites and cameras like we do today to make their theories abundantly clear even to the average person. The science finally overwhelmed the church's doctrine, and the church had to understand Scriptures about the corners and pillars of the earth as being metaphorical or poetic. They had to understand Scriptures that said the earth is immovable. They had to learn to interpret verses about the sun and moon encircling the earth as not being literal or scientific statements even though they described the scientific understandings of their day.

Has all this ultimately caused us to lose regard for the Scriptures? Or to say the Scriptures were wrong? No. We have learned to take it in stride, because we now know and accept the facts of the universe as deciphered by Galileo and Copernicus. We have ceased to believe we must take literally the several biblical passages that describe the universe differently. This is the case for us today even though the church once thought its prior concepts of the universe were so important to a Christian understanding of creation that giving them up would betray faith in the Bible.

Today if people claim the earth is flat or that the earth is at the center and everything revolves around it, they are just thought to be crackpots or at least terribly ignorant. Imagine if the church were still fighting to hold onto these ideas as essential to faith, or even trying to get these views taught in the public schools as an alternative science. Can anyone doubt that clinging to a flat-earth view of science and the universe would actually become a serious impediment to the spread of the Christian faith? Many would still believe, despite all evidence, as a matter of faith. But millions would reject Christianity as hopelessly out of touch with reality.

A 6,000-YEAR-OLD EARTH?

Maybe we have come to another "flat earth" point in the debate between science and a completely literal interpretation of the Bible. The biggest problem isn't the creation story itself but the impossibly short time-line of a 6,000-year-old earth many literalists are holding on to—even as it is so unnecessary to biblical faith. Sam Harris, the atheist I mentioned earlier, makes a lot of hay off this argument to show how ignorant people of faith are. He notes that surveys show nearly half of Americans are creationists who therefore believe the earth is only 6,000 years old. I'd have to see how the survey was worded to know if that is accurate, but certainly there are millions who do believe the earth is only 6,000 years old.

In the first place there is not one verse in the Bible that gives a date for creation. There are no passages that claim the creation happened only 2,500 years before Moses or only 4,000 years before Jesus. The *only* thing this belief in a very young earth rests on is dates calculated by adding up all the various genealogies scattered at various places in the Bible. If we stitch all these generations together as though the lists were comprehensive rather than representational lists, we arrive at about 4,000 years total before Christ. Only by treating these lists and numbers as though they were meant to answer contemporary questions of history and time do we create this problem at all. If we didn't think we had to accept this incredibly short timetable as a biblical truth, a great deal of the conflict between what we *know* about human history and the Bible story would be eliminated.

The genealogies from Adam to Noah in Genesis 5 provide ages when each father had a son. All of the other genealogies scattered around the Bible list only names and leave us to insert an average age to create a time-line and a date for creation. The only comprehensive genealogy, which is in Luke 3, lists ancestors from Jesus to Adam. Matthew 1 gives a list from Jesus back to Abraham and notes there were 14 generations from Abraham to David, 14 from David to the Babylonian captivity, and 14 from the Babylonian captivity to Jesus–a total of 42 generations between Jesus and Abraham. The list in Luke is a completely different line back to David.

Luke and Matthew even list different fathers for Joseph, whom both writers list as the father of Jesus. This is appropriate since Joseph followed the rules for adoption when he married Mary and named the child (Matt. 1:25). So Joseph was the legal father of Jesus although Mary was a virgin. I've heard suggestions that one of the writers may have actually traced the lineage through Mary and listed her father. However, both writers claim to be giving the lineage of Joseph, "the husband of Mary'" according to Matthew; and Luke says, "[Jesus] was the son, so it was thought of Joseph, the son of Heli. . . ."

But the biggest discrepancy between these two genealogies is that Luke lists 42 generations from Jesus to David, compared to Matthew's 42 generations from Jesus to Abraham! There were at least 800 years between David and Abraham. They can't both be 42 generations before Jesus, even by different lineages. This alone gives us a clue as to how literally we should take the genealogies. Might they be more representational than literal? Might the writers have simply intended to show there was a historical connection rather than to give us a historically accurate genealogy?

Besides the weak leg to stand on the genealogies offer, I have to wonder if people have really given serious thought to what a 6,000-year-old earth means. In addition to all the evidence we have to ignore to believe in a 4,000 BCE creation, is anyone thinking about the implications of a flood in about 2,500 BCE that wiped out all humanity except Noah's family? Human history starts over from scratch at that point. The problem is that this is not in pre-historic times. We have written records of entire civilizations at that time. As Sam Harris the atheist pointed out, we know who the pharaohs in Egypt were at that time. We know the names of emperors and dynasties in China at that time. We know the kings of Sumer and other Middle Eastern cities. All of these were in place and are historically connected to a continuous line of pharaohs and emperors and kings. There are breaks between some dynasties or kingdoms, but no sudden break in all in these histories around 2,500 BCE. Harris is absolutely right about this point.

Even if we ignore these written historical records, how can one account for all the races or ethnic groups of people of the entire earth evolving from one family in only one or two thousand years? The many peoples of Asia and Africa, Australia, the Arctic, native Americans, Europeans, Polynesians, the list goes on and on—all of these peoples were established as distinct ethnic and racial groups certainly by the time of Christ. If we reject evolution, how can we account for the wide array of the human race spread to every corner of the earth in the span of only forty or fifty generations?

I have to wonder if most people who claim to believe the earth is only 6,000 years old have actually thought about the implications of history beginning over in 2,500 BCE. They could give up this contradiction with known history and still keep believing the stories of the creation and the flood. If Christians understood the genealogies in a less literal way, all of the early Genesis events would be pushed back into the dawn of time and history. A 6,000 year old universe, with its accompanying 4,500-year-old human history since the flood is pretty close to a flat earth in terms of all the evidence against it. However, what exactly happened at the very dawn of the earth's creation is still a question even for scientists; a worldwide flood thousands of years before recorded history is certainly a possibility.

MAKING SCIENCE FIT WITH GENESIS

That isn't to say there aren't problems with a literal reading of the creation story of Genesis 1 as well. Some creationists have tried to make adjustments for what we know to be true. They have tried to make the creation story fit with some of the more obvious findings of science by suggesting that a "day" in Genesis may mean a "thousand years" (2 Pet. 3:8), or a million, or an age.

Some have taken a different tack by speaking of "intelligent design": Our beginnings at the least were not caused by random chance but required a higher intelligence to design the process. The scientific evidence points to a design of living things so complex at every level that it could not have come about by random interplay of the physical laws of our universe. Therefore there had to be an intelligent designer behind the process. Persons committed to intelligent design see an irreducible complexity at the genetic level that the mechanisms of evolution simply could not have been able to bring about by chance or even millions of chances. I'm not a scientist but the argument itself makes sense.

There may well be reason for scientists to disagree about the mechanisms of evolution for explaining all of life. I'm just not aware of any scientists who support the idea of intelligent design who weren't first *looking* for proof of a creator. The intelligent design argument or theory, however, doesn't depend on a Genesis 1 narrative. At its simplest it maintains that in some way, whether through evolution or another process, there was an intelligence guiding the process. Scientists complain that just to declare that a higher intelligence was necessary to plan all the complexity isn't science at all but a veiled statement of faith. I don't agree. Let me use another example.

Astronomers are trying to find any signs of other higher intelligence in the universe. So they beam radio signals out into space with messages in the hope of making contact. With giant dish receivers they listen to all the radio waves and other radiation coming at us from across the vast stretch of the cosmos. So far they have only heard random static and crackling.

The problem is, if we did hear a message from maybe fifty light years away, it would take fifty years to reply and another fifty to hear back. And that's from one of the close stars! But if one day we heard a real pattern that was complex language, a mathematical formula, or a symphony, or something else more complex than random noise, these scientists would be ecstatic. It would be proof that some intelligent being had sent that message however long ago or far away.

There could be disputes. Some might think it proved intelligence and more skeptical scientists might offer hypotheses as to how this could have happened naturally and randomly. They would need to hear something more complex. But at some point of complexity everyone would be convinced. We might still not have the slightest clue as to what or who had sent the message, but we would all agree it wasn't just an accident, because that would be statistically and mathematically impossible.

Intelligent design scientists studying DNA say we are at that point of complexity. Even if we can't know who that intelligence is or was, some intelligent being had to design this level of complexity. I believe that myself. The knowledge we have gained about DNA and cell structure has led us to realize that living cells are far, far more complicated than earlier scientists like Darwin himself ever imagined. They are not just a bunch of chemicals put together in just the right conditions that they came to life.

We have come a long way in cloning and manipulating the stuff of living cells, but I haven't seen anything to suggest we are getting nearer to creating a cell from non-living chemicals. My faith statement is that I believe the designer was God. Even if absolute proof were found to show evolution could have happened simply through the natural laws of the universe, I would still believe God had designed those natural laws in the first place.

Most people in the Christian church would agree with a belief grounded in their faith that a creator God is behind our design. It seems to me, however, that many Christians appeal to intelligent design simply in a thinly disguised attempt to discredit evolution—as though undermining evolution would validate the creation story, which for them is a foregone conclusion. "Creation science" starts with the Genesis story as a conclusion and then picks and chooses only the evidence that fits their conclusion.

Many Christians seem to assume that the theory of evolution is the biggest conflict between science and the Genesis account of creation. Far more basic to the foundations of science, and largely ignored, is the Genesis claim that the sun was created on the fourth day, three days after light and darkness and day and night, "evening and morning," and a day after plants were created.

The only explanation for this that I have heard from creationists is that *from the earth* the sun didn't appear through the heavy clouds until the fourth day. Obviously there were no eyewitnesses on the ground to have observed this anyway. If the only witness was God, who then revealed how the earth was created to the writer of Genesis, he wasn't limited to the perspective from the earth.

We know today that daylight results from the earth turning on its axis to face the sun which lights up the whole atmosphere. The sun *causes* daylight. But the story as told fits much better with the pre-scientific worldview of the time it was written. It reflects the science and cosmology of early Mesopotamia. Had the story been told to fit a modern scientific view it wouldn't have made sense to the people who first read it.

LOOKING AT THE STORIES THEMSELVES

For a long time I also ignored all the historic and scientific evidence and just believed that with God *anything* is possible. But I found the biggest problem with a literal understanding of the Genesis 1 creation story wasn't with science. It was the Genesis stories themselves that convinced me to understand the writer in a different way. When we actually read the accounts in Genesis 1-3, we find not one but *two* distinct creation stories. The first story goes from Genesis 1:1 through 2:3. Then Genesis 2:4 says, "This is the account of the heavens and the earth when they were created"—and a new account begins.

The first story begins with chaos and darkness across the water. Then God brings light and separates light from darkness into day and night. Next God creates a sky to separate the water above the earth from the water on the earth. God then separates land from water into seas and dry land, and plants appear. Now the sun, moon, and stars are created and finally the animals and humans. This story builds progressively to the pinnacle of the creation of man and woman. All of this is created by God's spoken command, *"Let there be...."* Finally God creates the Sabbath.

Some scholars believe Genesis 1 is a poem because of its repetitive structure. Hebrew poetry tends to repeat certain phrases, like the Psalms with repeating phrases like " . . . For his mercy endures forever . . . for his mercy endures forever ...," or " ... Praise ye the Lord ... praise ye the Lord. ... " Genesis 1 keeps repeating, "There was evening and morning, the first day. ... There was evening and morning, the second day. ..." It also keeps repeating that "God saw that it was good." So the first story is more of an epic poem of creation.

The second story begins on dry and barren land before there were any plants or bushes growing, and God kneels in the dirt, forms a man, and breathes life into him. Then God creates plants of all kinds in a garden and puts the man there. God makes all the animals also from the dust and finally a woman for the man. Then the story continues and tells how sin came into the world.

Just reading with no preconceptions, each account seems to be a separate story with a different form. Most revealing is something we hardly notice in our English translations of these Hebrew stories. In the first story God is referred to as *Elohim* and in the second as *Yahweh*. The English translators use "God" in the first account and "the LORD God," in the second. If one writer wrote both chapters, why would he have changed the name of God from the first account to the second?

Both the structure of the stories and the different names for God suggest two different sources for these stories. Genesis 2 does not read as simply the continuation of Genesis 1 or the story of the second week. It's not a retelling in abbreviated form of the same story.

When I realized all this, I could only conclude that the biblical evidence itself suggests Genesis 2 is a second creation story. This suggests the compiler of Genesis chose to include both stories because each reveals important truths about God and creation.

At the very least this raises the question of why one should choose the first account to take literally and ignore the sequence of the second account.

What were the sources for these accounts? Many Bible scholars agree that these stories were oral traditions long before they were written down. The stories were passed down from generation to generation until finally written. Both affirm that God created us and everything else. So why does the compiler of Genesis choose to include both stories without any attempt to harmonize them? That he includes both tells us *he wasn't going for historic or scientific accuracy*. Both were good stories that made different points, and both tell us some truth about God, about our creation, and about ourselves.

With our modern mindset we have a hard time thinking of something as being true unless it actually happened as told. Is the story of the Prodigal Son true? It is true that Jesus told it. But did it actually happen? As far as we know, it didn't. Yet it is a true story of God's love and grace. But of course Jesus tells us it is a parable, so in that way we also know it didn't actually happen. In contrast, the writer of Genesis doesn't tell us the story is figurative or metaphorical or poetic. We have to discover this by noticing two different stories of different origins that name God differently. We might also notice the difference between the ancient story and what we have since discovered about the history and age of our universe.

There are also various descriptions of the creation scattered throughout the Psalms—Psalms 8, 19, 29, 33, and 104 to name a few. We more easily accept these descriptions as poetic rather than literal because they are Psalms. At one time passages like Psalms 104:5 were taken quite literally as well—"He set the earth on its foundations; it can never be moved" was believed to be contradicted, as I noted at the beginning of this chapter, by Copernicus and Galileo who believed the earth did not stand still but revolved around the sun. When the evidence of a round earth, and of the earth and other planets revolving around the sun became incontrovertible, the church finally came to understand that those verses about corners and pillars of the earth, although they reflected the cosmology of the ancient world, must be understood today as metaphorical.

THEN WHAT DO THE CREATION STORIES MEAN?

If the creation stories in Genesis are not literal historical events, we are still left with the question of how to understand these stories and the question of how creation did take place. Essentially the source of our origins is one of the great un-knowables. The other unknowable is our end. Here again the Bible writers strive to explain or describe the end in the apocalyptic language of Revelation, which we also do well not to interpret too literally. Clearly the Bible calls us to remain faithful and to keep trusting God to guide the future to his ends, but the book of Revelation is hardly a clear roadmap of the future.

As for our beginnings, we are assured once again that God guided and caused our creation for God's purposes. Though the events themselves may be hidden from our view in the mists of an ancient past, we can try to describe what we understand or what our faith has taught us, as those who first told the creation stories of Genesis 1 and 2. Or we can look at evidence and propose scenarios, and as new evidence is found revise our scenarios, but there were no witnesses. Every civilization tries to give meaning to their origins and to their world. Most of these epic stories are tied to the transcendent and involve their gods. Quite a few of these stories are about struggles or battles of the gods—about death and birth.

Israel's stories in Genesis are unique among such narratives. Their stories tell of a God who simply speaks the world into existence. There is no struggle, or battle, or birth pangs. The second story is of a very personal God who kneels in the dirt and forms a man, and cares for him, and provides for him—a garden, animal companions, and finally a human companion—a woman. This God walks with these first humans in the cool of the evening and converses with them. The God of these stories is both all-powerful, as told in Genesis 1, and very personal and near at hand, as told in Genesis 2. We need both stories to complete a picture of God who is both transcendent and omnipotent but also immanent and personal.

The fact that these stories are told from the viewpoint or worldview of ancient Middle Eastern people does not weaken the powerful statements they make about God and our origins. Like a poem or a song, these stories strive to express the indescribable and the transcendent—that which we can only "see through a glass darkly."

We do a disservice to the stories when we woodenly force them to answer contemporary questions of scientific and historical accuracy. The purpose of the stories of Genesis, passed down from generation to generation and finally written down, was never to answer modern scientific or historical questions. They were answers to faith questions told in words that reflected their view of their cosmos. We would do well to tell a story as filled with faith in a God of creation to fit the historic and scientific views of our time. The scientific theory in vogue today suggests a big bang, in which all the matter and energy of the entire cosmos suddenly exploded from a very small spot. In essence everything suddenly appeared from nothing—*creatio ex nihilo!*

The evolution/creation debate has been pumped up to be an epic battle between the forces of true believers and secularists. This has become for some Christians an argument about ultimate meaning. Either we accept the creation story as literal fact or we must accept that we are simply an accident of nature whose life is meaningless.

This is a false dichotomy. We aren't limited to these two extreme positions. There are many shades between the literal creationist and the naturalist evolutionist who sees our design as simply the outcome of accidental, unfeeling natural causes. Those who believe in a God who created us can also believe that the God of creation is the God of all science and of the natural world with its many wonders. However we came to be, and through whatever process, God planned and created it all. All of our science, wherever it takes us, and without preconditions, is ultimately about discovering how God did it.

STANDING AGAINST THE WORLD'S WISDOM

Wouldn't it be better if all this energy to define ourselves against the prevailing culture really mattered? By that I mean this: At the end of the day, what real difference in my life does it make if I believe in one theory or the other about my origins? We can make all kinds of supposed important connections. But does it in any way make us better people, kinder people, more godly people for that matter? What if we chose to draw the lines along truly important distinctions? What if our point of reference for what defines us and sets us apart as Christians began and ended with Jesus Christ?

Some of us say, "I don't care what science teaches; I choose to believe the Bible no matter how contrary it might be to all the scientific learning in the world." What if instead we said, "I don't care how the world (and much of the church) tells us we must treat our enemies to be secure; I choose to believe Jesus, who tells us to love our enemies and to return good for evil, no matter how contrary that is to all the world's common wisdom?" That *would* make a real difference in the kind of people we are. It would make us kinder, gentler, and more Christ-like. We might be a cross-bearing people, but we would definitely differentiate ourselves from the world's culture of violence and power and revenge.

In October 2006, Charles Roberts walked into an Amish one-room school in Nickle Mines, Pennsylvania, and shot ten Amish girls, killing five in cold blood. He then shot himself. Almost immediately the Amish response was to forgive the killer. Not only did they say they forgave him, but some of the Amish community attended his funeral to grieve with his wife. When several million dollars were contributed to the families, they chose to share the funds with the killer's widowed wife. The whole world sat up and took notice of this extraordinary act of grace and forgiveness. The whole world saw Christ reflected in the actions of the Amish community. Their witness changed people's lives.

In a Mennonite Central Committee chapel talk (Jan. 8, 2009, Akron, Pa.) Ken Sensenig told four stories of lives changed by the example of the Amish of Nickel Mine. In one story, a prisoner in the Stony Mountain Penitentiary in Manitoba heard about the way the Amish forgave. He was baffled by the whole concept. As a gang enforcer his life was bent toward revenge and settling scores. When a Mennonite involved in a prison ministry visited him in prison, the prisoner kept asking him about forgiveness. The prisoner told him about his brother who had just died from a drug overdose. A cousin sold him the drugs, and since he was on medication for diabetes, the drugs killed him.

The cousin who had assured the prisoner's brother that the drugs were safe was now afraid for his life. He was sure that when the prisoner was released that he would be killed.

Now the prisoner was asking about forgiveness. The visitor brought the man a book on forgiveness and a Bible. When he returned to visit the prisoner later, the prisoner had read the book on forgiveness and was reading the Bible. He had decided to forgive his cousin and to become a Christian. He told his family to let his cousin know he had forgiven him.

What an amazing story of a transformed life through the example of a forgiving community of believers.

Chapter Seven

C. S. LEWIS ONLY HALF-BELIEVED IN NARNIA

C. S. Lewis is a beloved Christian writer respected by millions of Christians. I like most of what he wrote, but he wrote one essay with which I deeply disagree. This chapter is about that.

In his fantasies, *The Chronicles of Narnia*, C. S. Lewis inhabited a world imagined as wondrous—where good prevailed and evil was vanquished. Unlike the real world where evil often sits upon the throne unimpeded, he dared to imagine a world where brave and loyal creatures do battle to restore the rule of the righteous. Through the guise of fantasy and storytelling Lewis explored Christian theology. In a modern era and even now in the postmodern, he unpacked the "mysteries of the faith," and made them believable to many.

I have to wonder if his popularity is due to the fact that he challenges us at the philosophical and metaphysical level but not at the physical. There is a paradox in this because the very nature of fantasy suggests that there is a greater truth or a deeper reality behind the physical world we see. But Lewis only half-believed in that greater reality himself.

The half he believed in was the part it costs little to believe. It costs nothing to believe that after we pass from this earthly existence we enter into an eternal life with a loving God. In fact that brings us great comfort. It costs us little to believe Jesus "was born of a virgin, suffered and died, rose to life, and ascended into heaven from whence he will come to judge the quick and the dead."

There are those who scorn such beliefs but also ample millions who support rather than scorn those who do believe them. And it costs little to hold to a lot of other theological beliefs about redemption and forgiveness and salvation. All of that gives us great comfort.

Jesus also imagined and believed in a world where good prevailed and evil was vanquished—except not through heroic battles but through relinquishing everything to follow the way of the cross. To really believe there is a greater reality behind the physical reality we see and feel is to be ready to let it go. Jesus said that those who save their life will lose it, and any who lose their lives for the sake of his kingdom will save it. Jesus imagined a world where those with two coats would share with those who had none, where people would freely give to those who asked without expecting a return. Why? Because the physical things of this age just aren't something to hold on to.

Jesus imagined a forgiving reconciling community in which forgiveness actually costs something. We forgive in the same way God's grace comes to us, not because we deserve forgiveness, but because we need it so desperately. Jesus believed in a world where his followers would love everyone, even their enemies, because they were reconciled to all people. He believed in a kingdom where evil is conquered not with the sword but through the cross—the cross Jesus calls us to bear as well. Jesus saw that the real battle was not *against* evil people but *for* them. Only through the cross could those captivated by evil and addicted to power and violence be freed.

How could Jesus take such a leap of faith into the unknown? Because he really believed in that deeper reality beyond all worlds and beyond all seeing. Jesus saw that when we hate or destroy another, the very fabric of our existence is torn. The world remains broken, and our relationship to God is broken as well. That is the part of the deeper reality of our human existence where believing actually costs us something.

Since Jesus counseled those wanting to follow him to count the cost, isn't this an important test of true discipleship? Does it cost anything? It's the part C. S. Lewis seems not fully to believe in. He wrote an essay titled "Why I Am Not a Pacifist." He doesn't quote Jesus or Scripture even once but resorts to "common sense" and natural law (how the world operates—dog-eat-dog). His common sense of course is just another way of saying what the rest of the world believes. Lewis is firmly grounded in this world, with no argument from a deeper reality beyond this age. Essentially he argues that if we don't engage in wars to destroy evil foes, they will win and many people will suffer. If we don't resort to violence to save others we are complicit in their suffering.

Don't you suppose that argument occurred to Jesus as well? Israel suffered terribly under Roman oppression. Its people longed to be free. If Jesus died how would that possibly help those who were suffering? In fact the Romans did destroy Jerusalem and scatter the Jews just a few short years later. But Jesus believed in a deeper and older reality. He entrusted himself to God who worked with a bigger picture and was obedient even unto death.

Remember what Donald Miller said? I quoted him earlier from *Blue Like Jazz:*

> If we are created beings, the thing that created us would have to be greater than us, so much greater, in fact, that we would not be able to understand it. It would have to be greater than the facts of our reality, and so it would seem to us, looking out from within our reality, that it would contradict reason. (p. 201)

Certainly the challenge to lay down one's life to save it does seem to contradict reason.

But C. S. Lewis' argument is pretty much how most of the Christian church, as well as the secular world, approaches the issue of war and the use of violence. One of the obvious examples of most Christians not following Jesus is their response to his unambiguous words about loving our enemies. They believe that what Jesus says isn't practical, doesn't work, doesn't apply to this dispensation (as if loving our enemies would apply to the next age when we will have no enemies to love), or Jesus didn't mean it that way.

I've heard Christians say, as if it were just self-evident, that of course Jesus wasn't suggesting we shouldn't defend ourselves. He wasn't? Then what can he mean when he tells us to turn the other cheek if we are slapped? His words seem to me pretty plain and straightforward. Everything Jesus told his followers about loving enemies was said against the constant backdrop of the Roman occupation of Israel's land. When Jesus suggested going a second mile with the bags of a despised occupation soldier such as every patriotic Jew would want to throw out of Israel, his listeners understood he was talking about their enemies. They understood that when Jesus urged that they pray for those who were persecuting them (Matt. 5:38-44), he wasn't just talking about the next door neighbors who were aggravating them. Of course Jesus meant national enemies and not just our personal relationships—except Jesus had a way of making his relationships even to Roman soldiers and Samaritans personal.

Despite Jesus' clear unambiguous words, most Christians still don't believe they apply to war, to self defense, or even in civil cases. "Love your enemies" is just assumed not to work or to be realistic in a sinful world.

Fighting for religious freedom

Christians keep emphasizing the debt we owe to all those who have died so we can have the freedom to worship. In the first place our freedom is in Christ; we are always free to worship him even if that entails a cross. Jesus tells us to expect no less. But, in the second place, the claim that American soldiers died to protect our freedom to worship is simply not historically true. Which war did we fight for religious freedom? The Revolutionary War was fought for freedom from British rule and British taxes. Americans already had religious freedom here. People came to America over a hundred years before the Revolutionary War to have religious freedom or to escape religious persecution, but it wasn't something anyone here fought for.

The War of 1812 was a continuation of that conflict. The Mexican war was a simple land grab from Mexico. The Civil War freed the slaves but was hardly about religious freedom. All the Indian wars were genocidal campaigns to take Native American land. The Spanish American war was about extending American power. The two World Wars were largely about who would control Europe and the Pacific, not primarily about our religious freedom. And the Korean and Vietnam wars were touted as wars against communism, which is an atheistic political system, but neither war was against a real threat to our religious freedom. One *could* argue that the fall of Hitler and the fall of communism have brought more religious freedom to people in other countries

Finally the Central American and Iraq wars are again not about protecting our religious freedom but arguably about our economic interests. Christians in Iraq today are *more* persecuted under a Muslim-controlled government than they were even under the secular regime of Saddam Hussein. So why do we keep crediting our wars for our religious freedom?

HOW DID VIOLENCE BECOME THE "REALISTIC" SOLUTION?

Often those who work for nonviolent solutions are considered naïve, even though nonviolent movements have a far better track record of durable, real political change over the last fifty years. The outcomes of any of our wars during that period—Korea, Vietnam, Central America, or Iraq—were largely problematic. War and violence were disastrous in Ireland where the fighting went on and on for centuries until the combatants finally gave up on the violence, which had brought them to a complete stalemate, and negotiated peace. In Palestine the fighting has gone on for over fifty years with no end in sight.

Compare the outcome of violence and war over the last fifty years to the nonviolent overthrow of ruthless dictators like Marcos in the Philippines, Pinochet in Chile, the ending of apartheid in South Africa, the triumph of Solidarity in Poland, and even the collapse of the Soviet Union, all of which just fell apart when enough people took to the streets. Most recently we have seen the collapse of dictators in Egypt and other Mideast countries through nonviolent means.

Still, many people see nonviolence and even peace negotiations as naïve, lacking the hardnosed resolve needed to deal with our enemies in real world terms. Conservative Christians seem especially supportive of military solutions to deal with any threats to our power and security, even though we are hard-pressed to demonstrate how our recent wars have made us more secure.

Our recent history suggests the use of nonviolence is often no more "unrealistic" than expecting violence to bring peace. Although I believe that is true, I need to emphasize that *effectiveness is not the ultimate criteria* for followers of Jesus. Jesus called Israel under Roman rule to love her enemies because God does. I believe Jesus also called Israel to renounce violence and love enemies because it was ultimately the only hope for Israel. Might it be the only hope for the world today?

Jesus saw how counterproductive violence is. He said those who take the sword will perish by the sword. He wept over Jerusalem and the disastrous outcome he foresaw for the violent path Israel was choosing: "If you, even you, had only known on this day what would bring peace—but now it is hidden from your eyes." He predicted the disaster that indeed befell Jerusalem within forty years—"They will dash you to the ground, you and the children within your walls. They will not leave one stone on another," because Israel missed "God's coming" and because they rejected not only Jesus but also the way of peace he called people to live (Luke 19:41-44).

Yet most Christians make no connection between what Jesus clearly says about the disastrous outcome of violence and our wars today. Their strong support for military solutions stands in stark contrast to what Jesus taught and demonstrated. It is hard to see how being a follower of Christ affects their thinking at all regarding violence and war. If anything they are more hawkish than non-Christians. Many point to Jesus saying that there will always be wars and rumors of wars to the end of time. It's as though anyone working for peace must not believe what Jesus said.

Christians don't feel at all that way about Jesus saying the way to destruction is broad and many will take that road. They do everything they can to save people from hell. Just because Jesus predicts something doesn't mean we shouldn't make every effort to save as many as we can from destruction or to do everything we can to decrease wars and rumors of wars and all the suffering they bring.

I wonder if the reason Christians support war and capital punishment is because they are determined to root out evil? The Pharisees also wanted to get tough with evil and stamp out evildoers. They were bent on judgment and punishment.

I'm uncomfortable when I hear Christians say, "Sin is real and needs to be dealt with severely," not because I don't think sin is serious, but because it often gets translated into, "*sinners* need to be dealt with severely," which doesn't sound much like Jesus. This dark attitude toward human nature stands in contrast to the open and forgiving grace of Jesus and the *Abba* Father he portrays in his parables and teaching. Jesus' words of judgment were reserved for those who lacked compassion and mercy for people in need including sinners and tax collectors who were in need of a lot of grace and love.

LOVE BECAUSE GOD DOES

The Zealots of Jesus' day saw violence as the only way to overcome the Romans who ruled over them—often ruthlessly. Jesus had at least one or two Zealot disciples. He probably liked their zeal. He just never agreed with their violent agenda. Albert Nolan in his book, *Jesus Before Christianity*, proposes that Jesus showed no interest in a Jewish nation because he believed they would just be exchanging Roman oppression for Jewish oppression (see Appendix 2). Surprisingly Jesus also had a tax collector as a disciple. Tax collectors were considered Roman collaborators and traitors to Israel. The Zealots despised them. That Jesus had both Zealots and a tax collector in his band of disciples is a miracle in itself.

When Jesus said we are to love our enemies, his words stood in sharp contrast to the hatred of the Zealot freedom fighters who wanted to kill them. Jesus said we are to love our enemies to be the children of our Father.

Have you ever heard someone say, "He's a chip off the old block," or "She's just like her daddy"? Jesus says if we want to be like God, we have to love our enemies because that's what God does. God sends the sunshine and rain on good and bad people alike. God doesn't pick and choose between friends and enemies. So when Jesus says we are to be perfect as God is, he's talking about the nature of God's love which is perfect—undivided, unadulterated, undiscriminating, universal (Matt. 5:43-48). How else can we demonstrate God's love to the world?

If we are to love our enemies because God does, can we draw a conclusion that sometimes that might mean killing them? I understand that many sincere Christians believe Jesus was referring to our personal enemies and not national conflicts, although I don't agree with that. I also understand that some Christians feel love for our neighbor requires us to defend our neighbor even with deadly force if needed. But even if you believe that there are such circumstances, shouldn't faith in Christ compel us to set the bar high and rare? Instead it seems Christians are ready to jump into war as soon as the first bugle sounds.

Shouldn't there be *some* wars that Christians in a given country recognize for what they are and refuse to fight? If Christians say wars are sometimes justified, doesn't that imply some aren't? The church has set criteria for justified wars. Now every single government makes the case that every war fits the criteria (even if this is a total sham), and most of the church marches off to war.

Jesus must have been concerned for those suffering under a cruel Roman occupation. He certainly faced the expectation of those around him that he, as the Messiah, would do something about it. Nevertheless, he chose the path of the cross which he explicitly called us to follow as well.

Jesus ultimately didn't reject violence because it is too dangerous but because it is too weak. Violence never gets at the root of the evil we face. If our struggle isn't against flesh and blood, as Paul says in Ephesians, then people are not the enemy. Jesus' battle isn't against evil people but *for* them. How do you win someone back from the "dark side?" If you kill them, you just lost them to the real enemy.

BUT WHAT IF SOMEONE WAS GOING TO SHOOT YOUR FAMILY?

For several years a Catholic sister would have me talk to her ethics class in a girls' high school about pacifism. She wanted them to be exposed to other ways of thinking. The question that invariably came up was the hypothetical scenario—"You mean if someone broke into your home with a gun and was going to kill your family and you had a gun you wouldn't kill them to save your family?"

My response came to be, "Okay, let's go with that hypothetical situation. What if a guy came into *your* home with a gun and threatened to kill your family? Let's say your mother was home and she had a gun and knew she could surprise him and shoot him, but that was very hard for her to do because the young man with the gun was her son and your brother."

The look on the girls' faces suddenly changed at this twist, but I continued, "He may have become very angry and estranged from the family, but he's still her son. Does she kill him?

"That isn't to say some mothers wouldn't kill even their own son to save others in the family, but it would be a much more difficult decision. She couldn't just automatically blow him away. Most mothers would go to great lengths and take a lot of risk to themselves and their family to not have to kill him. Because he is her son and your brother."

Isn't that the point of what Jesus calls us to? Because our enemy *is* also our brother and our sister.

God's desire is for all his children to be reconciled, even those who are estranged from God's family. Paul says Jesus reconciled Jews and Gentiles, who were enemies, through his death on the cross, whereby he *"put to death their hostility"* (Eph. 2:14-17, emph. added). Jesus battle wasn't against the Gentiles *or* the Jews. His battle was against their hostility and estrangement from each other and from God. Jesus calls us to the same task of reconciliation to a broken world.

We are, Paul says, his ambassadors—representatives of a foreign kingdom—as though Christ was making his appeal through us to be reconciled to God and to each other (2 Cor. 5:18-20). Jesus not only calls us to the same task but to the same method—the way of the cross.

Even if you believe Jesus' call to love our enemies doesn't apply to war and self-defense, how can you get around Jesus' call to take up a cross and follow him? Jesus' clear expectation was that his followers would suffer for being his followers. His Way was the way of suffering. How can we square that expectation with fighting and killing to avoid suffering? Jesus' call to take up a cross must mean Christians should not expect to have the freedom we are so ready to kill to protect. The choice is always between the way of the cross or the sword. We can't choose both.

Doesn't Paul tell us to support our government?

Actually, most Christians don't argue with the things Jesus said; they just ignore them in favor of what they believe is "common sense," like C. S .Lewis and much of the church, or they go elsewhere in the Bible. Some point to the Old Testament wars God commanded, but Christians don't use the Old Testament as a full and literal guide in most other areas of their lives.

So more often they turn to Romans 13 where Paul talks about God ordaining governments to use the sword. Many interpret Romans 13 to mean we should obey and support the government. Actually it says to *"Be subject"* to the government, not obey. And you can only understand Romans 13 in light of its context. The text is sandwiched between passages calling the Christians in Rome to return good for evil, at the end of chapter 12, and to owe no one anything but love (Rom. 13:8). We need to remember that the Roman government was essentially hostile to both Christians and Jews. Both communities would have prayed for freedom from Rome, and there would have always been the attraction of Zealot-related groups dedicated to throwing Rome out of Palestine or seeing Rome overthrown altogether. So Paul's admonition to be subject to the government is written to a community wishing to throw off Roman persecution or oppression. Paul says that isn't the way of Jesus.

Remember Paul didn't write his epistles with chapters and verses. Scholars added them later. So if we read straight through from Romans 12:14 through 13:8 (I won't quote it all, but the thought flows like this), Paul tells these Christians to

> Bless those who persecute you . . . do not repay anyone evil for evil . . . as far as it depends on you, live at peace with everyone. Do not take revenge. . . . Do not be overcome by evil, but overcome evil with good. Let everyone be subject to the governing authorities. . . . The authorities that exist have been established by God. Consequently, whoever rebels against the authority is rebelling against what God has instituted. . . . Let no debt remain outstanding, except the continuing debt to love one another.

When you read across the part about overcoming evil with good and the very next phrase is a call to be subject to the governing authority, it sounds like the governing authority was itself an example of the evil to be overcome by good. Asking the Christian community not to rebel against an evil and often tyrannical government is a long way from telling Christians to take the government's side and fight her wars. To argue that Paul's words can be stretched to support our fighting for any government of this age is indeed a stretch.

Christ instead calls us to enter the reign of God. We pray God's will be done on earth as in heaven. We, as ambassadors of God's reign and God's kingdom among us already, are called to live in that reality. We can risk the way of the cross to overcome evil because we walk in the light of the resurrection.

Giving up our spears

When I'm driving alone in the car it helps me stay awake to listen to talk rather than music. So one day while driving I came across an interview with Steve Saint on a Focus on the Family program. Steve is the son of Nate Saint, one of five missionaries killed in 1956 by a tribe in the Amazon in Ecuador. Steve told how some of the missionary wives and his aunt Rachel Saint stayed in Ecuador after the men were killed to continue trying to reach this Amazonian tribe. His aunt Rachel lived with the tribe for thirty-nine years. The effect on the tribe of these women continuing to reach out to them even after they had killed their husbands and brother was profound. Many became Christians because of the women's demonstration of forgiveness.

Steve was a young boy when his father was killed, and as I remember from the radio show he went to school somewhere else but spent summers with his aunt Rachel in the village. He told two stories from that period. One day a man in the tribe who had helped kill the missionaries was talking to Rachel about Steve. He was very concerned about the boy because he felt Steve didn't know anything he needed to survive in the jungle. He didn't know how to track animals and hunt. He couldn't make poison darts. What would become of a boy who couldn't even take care of himself? Rachel told the man, "Well who is going to teach him? You killed his father."

The man went away and returned the next day to tell her that since he had killed the boy's father, it was his responsibility to teach Steve how to hunt and survive. So he did just that. What a story of reconciliation and restitution.

The other story unfolded when Steve was nine years old. He stayed with Rachel in her hut. They both slept in hammocks. One night he heard a lot of yelling and shouting outside. He woke Rachel and asked what was going on. She sat up in her hammock and listened to all the shouting for awhile. Then she told him it was another tribe across the river shouting threats over to their tribe. But their tribe was shouting back, "Even if you do spear us, we don't spear people anymore." Rachel rolled over and went right back to sleep. Eventually the shouting died down and the other tribe left.

The implication of Steve's story was that the tribe had gotten the Christian message of love and forgiveness; therefore its members were no longer willing to kill anyone. The story left a question in my mind. When a tribe gets big enough to be a nation, does that message of love and forgiveness no longer apply?

Will we place our trust in the cross or our "spears?" We can't embrace both because they are opposite ways of dealing with evil. To take up a spear is to reject the cross as our own calling. The tear in the very fabric of the universe is only healed through the ongoing work of the cross. Evil is only defeated through the cross. This war we are called to wage is led, not by a lion, but a slain lamb. The purpose of the war is not to destroy the enemies of God but to redeem them back into God's family. We are followers of that Lamb, and the victory is assured. *"Peace I leave with you; my peace I give you. I do not give to you as the world gives. Do not let your hearts be troubled and do not be afraid"* —Jesus (John 14:27).

Chapter Eight

JESUS AND ISRAEL IN PROPHECY

Woe to you who long for the day of the Lord! Why do you long for the day of the Lord? That day will be darkness, not light.
—Amos 5:18

I've been thinking for a number of years that I'd like to write a novel about the end times. In my book Jesus would return. There would be a great battle at Armageddon. The forces of righteousness would of course win. The Muslim Dome of the Rock on the temple mount in Jerusalem would be destroyed and the temple rebuilt on that spot grander than ever before.

In the mopping-up phase, all those who refused to pledge their allegiance to the thousand-year reign of Christ from Jerusalem would be cast out and destroyed. But then Jesus would really return and reveal the previous "Jesus" as the anti-Christ. Because what many Christians are fully expecting at the second coming would be anti-Christ in so many ways.

The Jewish people were all expecting that when the Messiah came he would "redeem Israel," and they didn't just mean spiritual redemption; they expected the Messiah to re-establish the nation of Israel once again. He would destroy

the enemies of Israel, and Israel would become the great nation it had been under King David and even greater. If you
read Mary's song before Jesus birth, and what Simeon said
when he blessed the baby Jesus in the temple, they clearly
were looking for someone to restore Israel.

Up to the night Jesus was arrested, his own disciples,
who had been with him for three years, were still expecting
soon to be sitting next to Jesus ruling Israel. Before his ascen-
sion into heaven they were still asking, "Is this the time you
will restore Israel?" The non-restoration of Israel was probably the most significant reason Jesus was never recognized as
Israel's Messiah. *Everyone* in Israel understood the prophesies about the Messiah to mean Israel's restoration. Yet Jesus
never showed any interest in that hope.

It is no coincidence that Jesus' temptations in the wilder-
ness revolved around how he would carry out his mission as
God's Anointed. His temptations immediately followed the
voice from heaven at his baptism that confirmed him as
God's beloved son. His temptations were all temptations to
greatness and power.

The Bible says Jesus was tempted in every way like we
are, but do you know anyone who has had a face-to-face conversation with Satan? And have you ever been tempted to
worship Satan for any reason? I have never been tempted to
be a Satan worshipper, and I doubt Jesus was. If he was
tempted like we are, he would have been struggling with the
question of how he was to be Israel's Messiah. He would
have had to struggle with what *everyone* else expected and
try to figure out what God wanted. He must have struggled
with the thought of all the wonderful things he could do for
Israel if he were king. The struggle or confrontation was
within himself—but he understood the temptations to make
bread, or to perform a miraculous sign at the temple, or to
gain power over all the kingdoms of the earth as temptations
from Satan himself.

Later when Peter proclaims that Jesus is the Christ (the
Greek word for Messiah), Jesus commends him and then
adds that he will go to Jerusalem and be killed there. Peter
strongly rebukes Jesus, saying that can never happen (be-

cause it does not fit his understanding of the Messiah). Jesus says, "Get behind me Satan," thereby acknowledging once again a temptation from Satan himself. He tells Peter he is thinking like men think and not like God thinks (Mark 8:29-33).

Jesus asks what good it would do if he gained control of the whole world but lost his soul (Mark 8:36). Because while Peter and all of Israel are thinking about the prophesies of a conquering king, Jesus is thinking about the prophesies of a suffering servant. Jesus' followers are thinking how much they want to be free of the hated Romans; Jesus is telling them to love the very enemies who are persecuting them. They want to see Rome destroyed and Israel redeemed; Jesus wants to redeem the Romans as well.

Jesus understands that God loves the whole world. His mission is far larger than Israel alone. Jesus shows no interest in establishing the nation of Israel then or any time in the future. He never predicts or looks forward to that happening. He inaugurates a broader "kingdom of God" that encompasses all who believe in him and accept his reign. He doesn't set out to defeat the enemies of Israel.

So why are many Christians certain that when Jesus returns he will do all the things he refused to do the first time he came and lived among us? Isn't it because they are reading the very same prophecies and essentially interpreting them the *very same way* the Pharisees and Zealots and even Jesus' own disciples did? Oh, they have added new things to include Jesus—crucified, resurrected, and reigning with God.

But the prophecies about Israel being re-established, the Messiah conquering and slaying God's enemies—all the things Jesus refused to endorse when he walked the earth and proclaimed the reign of God—are often understood today much as the Pharisees and Zealots did. Many Christians still expect a great bloody battle of the forces of righteousness and the forces of evil, with the Messiah as a conquering king leading the charge in destroying the enemies of God to inaugurate a reign of peace from Jerusalem. And where do Christians find these images? The same place the

Jews of Jesus day found them—in the Old Testament prophets.

They also read the parts of Revelation that speak of a new Jerusalem and all the dire predictions. However, they miss the imagery in John's Revelation of a slain *Lamb* who conquers by the sword of his *mouth* (Rev. 2:16, 5:6). In the Pharisees' and Zealots' imagery *and* in dispensationalist imagery, the Messiah is spilling the blood of his enemies. Jesus demonstrated that his way is as the Messiah who sheds his own blood for his enemies and calls his faithful followers to the same path.

A NEW THEOLOGY OF THE END

Some of today's ideas about prophecy are actually quite new and different ways of understanding the Bible. The church, for example, never taught a dispensationalist view of prophecy with a rapture of the church before a time of tribulation, as laid out in the *Left Behind* series, until Darby in Britain, and then Scofield in the United States, figured out this whole new theory of prophecy less than 150 years ago. It has become widely accepted across a large swath of American Christianity. However, many other Christians (not just liberal scholars) and even fundamentalists do *not* embrace this view of prophecy with its pre-tribulation rapture, which is the whole premise of the *Left Behind* books.

The book *End Times Fiction* by Gary DeMar is written from a very conservative understanding of the Bible but finds no biblical basis for this theological point of view. DeMar points out that there is not a single verse in the Bible that places the rapture of the saved before a time of tribulation. The only mention of the rapture is in 1 Thessalonians 4:13-18, with no mention of a time of tribulation. Darby just decided to place the rapture before the tribulation.

John Nelson Darby from England and C. I. Scofield from Texas believed biblical prophecies called for the re-establishing of Israel in Palestine over fifty years before it happened. So when Israel became a nation again in 1948, many felt that dispensational premillennialism had been confirmed.

I remember reading that Lord Balfour, who signed a declaration calling for a homeland for Jews in Palestine, believed in Darby's view of prophecy as did Winston Churchill. Wanting to verify a source for this, I did a search and found that some researchers feel there is good evidence for a connection between Darby and Lord Balfour and even Churchill. Others have doubts. So were these British leaders who controlled Palestine at the time believers or at least sympathizers of dispensationalism and Christian Zionism who then brought about the fulfillment of these prophecies?

In any event many Christians, but certainly not all of them, believed Darby and Scofield were proved correct. These dispensationalists see a direct connection between the prophecies of the Bible and the founding of the nation of modern Israel. They read certain Scriptures taken from the books of Ezekiel, Daniel, Revelation, Thessalonians, the Gospels, and numerous other books. Then they put them all together into a single scheme as though all these books were written with clues in each that we are supposed to find and put together like a puzzle. (Of course all these puzzle pieces can just as well be put together to form different patterns. Hence all the various views of prophesy.)

By reading the Bible this way—a piece here and a piece there, and *only* in this way, they construct dispensationalist premillennialism, with a pre-tribulation rapture, and the rebuilding of the temple and the sacrificial system in Jerusalem in modern Israel. Millions of Christians have adopted this view and believe it is simply what the Bible teaches.

One version of the Bible does teach this view. Scofield created his own edition of a King James Version of the Bible in 1909, with copious footnotes all linked together to lead the reader from one verse to the next to show how it all fits together like a giant puzzle. The Scofield Bible sold in the millions.

I had a professor in seminary who told me he and his brother used to travel all around the country holding prophecy conferences. They had charts and graphs and illustrations to explain everything that was going to happen. I asked what had changed his beliefs about prophecy. He sim-

ply said, "I studied Hebrew." Once he read all those prophesies in the original Hebrew they would no longer bear the
weight of all the tortured interpretations he had read back
into them from his King James Bible.

The fundamentalist view of Scripture creates much of
the problem. Old Testament prophecies are declared to be
without error—so they must come to pass. This is in contrast
to Paul, who says that where there are prophecies, they will
cease, tongues will end, and knowledge will pass away, for
now we know in part and we prophesy in part, but when
perfection comes the imperfect passes away. Now we see but
a dim reflection and know only partly, but then we will know
fully, even as we're fully known (1 Cor. 13: 8-12).

Whether or not Paul was suggesting that some prophecies were imperfect, certainly our understanding of them is
imperfect. We can see this by all the differing and ever-
changing interpretations of what they mean. Yet how often
do preachers give the meaning of a particular prophecy and
declare it as God's unfailing word?

Dispensationalism was based on the idea that any
prophesy in the Bible that had not yet come to pass was still
to happen in the future. So every prophetic vision in the Bible
had to be tied into an overall framework of how the future is
yet to play out. One of the major difficulties of this way of
treating the Old Testament prophets is that it is completely
different than the way the Old Testament Law is treated.
Christians largely agree that the Law no longer applies to
Christians. It has been set aside through the work of Christ
on the cross, and we are no longer bound by the Old Testament Law. The apostle Paul says this emphatically.

VISIONS OF A JEWISH FUTURE

So why would we still be bound by the vision of the future foretold by the prophets of the Old Testament? Being
Jewish prophets their vision of the future was a Jewish vision. In a Jewish future all the elements of the Jewish faith are
front and center. When they foretold what God's plan would
be for the future of Israel, and indeed the whole world, that

future centered on Jerusalem and the temple. The prophets saw a future with the whole world streaming to Jerusalem to worship as Jews. They weren't imagining a future in which the sacrifices and the temple itself would be supplanted by the Messiah and his death on a cross. They foretold a Jewish future.

They did imagine a time in a perfect future when no one would need to be taught the Law anymore because it would be written on everyone's heart. Everyone would just naturally know and follow the Law (Jer. 31:33-34). The Jewish prophets never predicted the time would come that the Law would be done away with all together.

Jesus shows no interest in this Jewish vision of a restored and central Jerusalem with its temple worship. He tells the woman at the well, "The time is coming when you will worship the Father neither on this mountain nor in Jerusalem . . . a time is coming and has now come when the true worshipers will worship the Father in the Spirit and in truth" (John 4:21-24). Jesus predicted the destruction of the temple (Mark 13:1-2) and never suggested it would be rebuilt.

The apostle Paul never teaches the restoration of temple worship and an independent nation of Israel. Revelation describes the "new Jerusalem" coming down from heaven and encompassing the whole known world—a city 1,500 miles square and even 1,500 miles high to make a perfect cube as the Holy of Holies had been. The Holy of Holies in the tabernacle and later in the temple was the dwelling place of God. So although a city 1,500 miles high is probably not to be taken literally, it signals that the whole earth is to become the dwelling place of God with his people. And Revelation says specifically that in the new Jerusalem there will be no temple since God and the Lamb are its temple (Rev. 21:22).

Yet dispensational theology centers on the old vision of Israel and the temple being restored and blends that vision into the gospel of Christ even though Christ himself never taught that. If the Jewish Law with all its requirements has been set aside in Christ, hasn't the prophetic vision of a Jewish future been set aside as well? If the Law isn't God's infallible Law for all time, why are the Prophets?

Jesus predicted and the early church went on to apply all the promises God made to Israel to include any people around the earth who turned to the God revealed in Christ. Jesus said that God could raise up children of Abraham from the stones on the ground (Matt. 3:9). The epistles speak of our being grafted in to God's family and becoming heirs to the promises to Israel (Gal. 3:29, Eph. 3:6). The New Testament simply doesn't predict a rebirth of Israel as a nation—and certainly not as the secular nation it is today.

IS MODERN ISRAEL A FULFILLMENT OF PROPHECY?

If it weren't so pervasive an issue, I probably wouldn't have gotten into this discussion about prophecy because the apocalyptic books of the Bible are probably the most subject to all kinds of wild schemes and interpretations. Most of the really wacky cults have emerged from some strange interpretation of these books of prophecies and visions. Because of the symbolic language, they can be made to say almost anything. And arguments about how the world will end can become meaningless and speculative at best. But at worst they can be downright dangerous in real-world situations. Atrocities do happen in the name of fulfilling prophecy.

The name *Israel* means "one who struggles with God." Is there any way the nation of Israel today is putting faith and trust in God? Israel today is everything the prophets of old condemned: They trust in their military might instead of in God. They trample the rights of those outside their community. They have forgotten their call to be a blessing to all the peoples of the earth and have instead become, for over fifty years, an example of unrest and repression. To a large degree, the re-establishment of the nation of Israel demonstrates on the one hand both the power of modern weapons systems, good military strategy, and an alliance with the U.S., *and* on the other hand their futility in creating real peace. This is the tragedy of the dispensationalist view of prophecy and Christian or Jewish Zionism.

We need to recognize that after the Holocaust, Jews worldwide understandably longed for a homeland within which they could seek refuge from future such horrors. Yet how tragic it then is that, along with their allies, those who knew too well how humans can destroy each other could glimpse only an approach that created home for Jews by destroying home for Palestinians.

Jimmy Carter was strongly criticized for his book referring to Israel's policy toward the Palestinians as "apartheid." But what do you call it when a country has highways for Jews only, that go from Israel to settlements inside Palestinian territory in the West Bank? These highways aren't for Israelis only, because Arab Israelis aren't allowed on them either. They are only for Jews. This may well be because Israeli settlers feel threatened as intruders in Palestinian territory, but they have also aggravated the situation—sometimes purposely.

What do you call it when settlers can take over a hilltop in the West Bank on Palestinian land and set up temporary buildings or shipping containers and begin to live there under the protection of Israeli forces? These are recognized even by the Israelis as illegal settlements, but the settlers are often not forced to leave. More settlers move in. More buildings are moved in. After a while it is a recognized "fact on the ground" and becomes a recognized Israeli settlement that enters all the other "facts" that are unyielding or at least will create powerful negotiating points in any peace settlement. While peace talks drag on and start and stop, more illegal settlements go up—all under the watchful eye of the Israeli army. Always swallowing up more of what had been Palestinian land.

We hear all the terrible stories of Palestinian terror against innocent Israelis, but we often end up hearing less in our news sources about the harassment of Palestinians by Israeli soldiers and settlers. Christian Peacemaker Teams and other groups working in Israel and the West Bank have witnessed many instances of harassment and intimidation. These range from grade school children being harassed by settlers on their way to school to shots being fired from the Israeli settlement into nearby Palestinian homes so homeowners no longer dare live in the front part of their own homes. Israeli soldiers do little about these situations. Random shots: How can they know whom to arrest? So no one is arrested, of course. The soldiers usually take the side of the settlers.

Christian Peacemakers escorted the harassed schoolchildren, hoping the settlers would leave them alone if they were being watched. Israeli soldiers told the Peacemakers to stop the escorting. Israeli settlers even attacked the Peacemakers, and Israeli soldiers did nothing to intervene. There are many other stories of settlers harassing Palestinians in large and small ways. Few dare to protest because the Israeli soldiers nearby always side with the settlers.

Then there is the larger provocation of hundreds of Palestinian homes bulldozed for one reason or another—sometimes in response to a terror attack even though the homeowner had no connection with the bomber at all, sometimes to clear houses for "security reasons," sometimes because the house was built without proper permits. Never mind that the Palestinians are hardly ever issued building permits on their own property even as Israelis can get permits all the time.

Jewish neighborhoods have enough water for lawns but Palestinians often don't even have regular running water for bathing and cooking. When the Israelis have a legal system always weighted to their side, and when the security forces almost always take their side, and Israeli Jews have privileges not allowed for the Palestinians, isn't that the definition of apartheid? Israelis feel they were provoked into this policy, and they deserve our effort to understand their point of view. Yet the facts suggest that whatever the provocation, this is apartheid nevertheless. The policy seems to one of harassment that makes life so miserable Palestinians will get the message and leave, which is in fact what many have done.

This doesn't quite rise to the level of ethnic cleansing and certainly not genocide, which would be loudly condemned in the world community, including the Jewish community. I'm not sure, however, that genocidal policies would be condemned by some Christian Zionist dispensationalists. They are so sure that God wants Israel to occupy the whole land of ancient Israel that many would accept almost any means.

With such overwhelming repression, is it any wonder the Palestinians turned to terror as their only weapon? The tragedy of all this is that the Palestinians didn't consistently take the more difficult path of nonviolence. Violence begets violence, and terrorism removes any chance of widespread sympathy from the world community or from within the Jewish community itself.

I believe there would be a Palestinian nation today if Palestinians had refused all forms of violence. But like many Christians they bought into the myth that sometimes you have to use violence to protect your people. "Sometimes violence is the only thing the other side will understand." When in fact any violence, even throwing rocks at soldiers with machine guns, has given the Israelis the cover needed to continue their occupation and holds their American allies back from condemning them too strongly or even withholding aid. So we continue to support Israel with little protest.

In light of all the displaced and exiled Palestinian Muslims and Christians alike, there is finally something very incongruous about the way American fundamentalists read the apocalyptic writings of Daniel and John's Revelation. Apocalypses were written by and for the persecuted, the downtrodden, and the exiled, to give hope of vindication—that one day the tables will be turned. Remain faithful even though you are going through fierce trials. One day God will intervene and make things right. As Psalm 37 says,

> A little while and the wicked will be no more; . . . But the meek will inherit the land and enjoy peace and prosperity. . . . The wicked draw the sword and bend the bow to bring down the poor and the needy, to slay those whose ways are upright. But their swords will pierce their own hearts, and their bows will be broken. (vs. 10-15)

This was also the point of view of the apocalyptic writers.

Now churches in the most wealthy and powerful country in the world look forward to the day when the kingdoms of this age will be brought low—as if they weren't a part of that kingdom. At the same time these churches and their leaders are devising strategies for more power in the very kingdom they anticipate will soon fall. They call for the expansion of the military power of the most powerful country in the world. They fear any loss of power and prepare to take on any challenge while looking forward in anticipation to the day when all governments will fall and the powerful will be brought low. Don't they get it?

Chapter Nine

SEX EDUCATION AND INERRANCY

I'm writing this chapter to share my understanding of the Bible and inspiration. I want to be as clear as I can about where I'm coming from. I've already alluded to some of my beliefs about Scripture and how it is often misused. Some of my ideas are in process, and I'm not dogmatic about them. So I share this not to convince you of my view, because I believe true Christians range across a wide spectrum of beliefs on many doctrines, including inspiration. What I am dogmatic about and hope to influence Christians about, is the centrality of Jesus to all our understandings of God and the Scripture. With that let me share how my thoughts have developed.

For me a moment of thinking differently about the nature of the Bible had to do with sex education. I looked at the Bible essentially as though it had been written by God himself, actually dictated by God. I was taking an Old Testament course in college. There were other more liberal students who thought the creation stories were myths (in the best sense of the word). I believed the stories were true, although I thought each day of creation might well have covered thousands of years and been much longer ago. I was bothered by the idea that the sun was only created on the fourth day, after the plants on the third day, and well after the dividing of light from darkness—day and night—on the first day. But I accepted that, even though I couldn't *explain* how the story could be true, nothing was impossible for God. So I just chose to believe it.

Then we were required to read all of the first five books of the Bible—the Torah. So I was plowing through Genesis and the first parts of Exodus which had some very interesting stories, then I got into a lot of details about the construction and design of the tabernacle, all the rules for priests in Leviticus, the long tribal family lists of Numbers, and even more explicit details of law in Deuteronomy.

I was a little disturbed by the severity and strictness of the Law that God gave to Moses. There were so many reasons for stoning people to death, including if a son was disobedient to his parents, or if a young couple had sex before marriage. I saw these as common occurrences, and although they were wrong, hardly deserving of death. I decided that the God of the Old Testament must have been really serious about eliminating even ordinary sins. So although God seemed to me to have been excessively strict, and hardly the picture of the God of grace and forgiveness of the New Testament, I was in no position to judge God or God's justice. This was the God of the Law before grace came to us through Jesus' death for our sins.

Then I came to Deuteronomy 22:13-21. Here the Law commanded that if a man married a young woman and found on their wedding night that there was no blood on the sheets to indicate the girl was a virgin, he was to take the bedding to the elders and the girl's parents as proof she was not a virgin. She was therefore to be stoned.

Being in college, I had a lot of curiosity about the mysteries of sex and had read *Everything You Always Wanted to Know About Sex, but Were Afraid to Ask,* so I knew that although it was a popular belief that virgins always bleed the first time they have intercourse, that doesn't always happen. So now I started to wonder if God was not only overly strict but unfair as well. If young women don't always bleed the first time they have sexual intercourse this was not a fair test of virginity. Furthermore God would know this.

I knew at that moment that God had not written (or dictated) those words. I decided that men in all sincerity and with a holy zeal to weed out evil among them had written that command thinking they were administering God's justice. But it wasn't God. God could do anything, no matter how miraculous or unexplainable by science, God could be far stricter in His justice than I liked, though what should be done was God's decision to make, not mine. But God could not be unjust nor ignorant of sexual physiology and anatomy. I had to either change my concept of God as a God of justice and love or change my concept of the Bible and how it came to us. I changed my view of the Bible.

SO WHAT IS INSPIRED?

That didn't mean for me that the Old Testament wasn't inspired. I just needed to come to a different understanding of what that now meant. Clearly the history of Israel was infused with God's presence. Abraham and Moses and many others were inspired by God or they wouldn't have done what they did. So these are God stories. The people of the Old Testament were inspired by God and responded in faith. We see all these heroes of faith along with all their faults. Like the rest of us, these people of faith neither heard nor followed perfectly. Moses wasn't infallible, and the Old Testament never claims he was. It follows then that the writing of these stories is not infallible either.

How was God at work in the Old Testament, if not in the writing of every word? If we decide one part does not reflect the true will of God, does every part become questionable? So is any part of the Bible a reliable authority? The short answer to the last question is really very simple. The fullest and most authoritative word we can rely on is The Word—Jesus. He said, if we have seen him, we have seen God. Jesus doesn't call us to follow the Bible; he calls us to follow him. Jesus is the final revelation of God—God's "Word" to humankind lived out among us. Wherever we see a picture of God that is at odds with or different from the God revealed in Jesus, we can know that view of God is incomplete—what

Paul meant when he said, "Now we see through a glass darkly." In Christ we see God—*face to face.*

Several people have questioned me on this principle. Then how can I trust Jesus if the only thing I know about Jesus is what the Bible says? If the Old Testament isn't reliable, how can I trust what the New Testament says about Jesus? My questions about the Old Testament's historical stories aren't about their accuracy but their understanding of God, which is a changing understanding. I believe the stories *accurately reflect* what Abraham, Moses, David, Isaiah (and all the rest) did and what they believed God was saying to them. In the same way I believe the Gospels accurately tell us what Jesus did and taught.

The Bible is God's story—the story of God's relationship with his people. Although the Bible does have some theological passages that tell us propositional truths about God, primarily we learn about God through God's relationship or interactions with people. When we use the Bible to prove this or that theological point about God, we often end up going further than the Bible does. Maybe God isn't so interested in theological positions or religious rituals. God wants to be involved in all our everyday lives broken as we are.

When I saw that Abraham and all the others stepped out in faith with what they understood—imperfect as that was—God used and blessed their faith despite their failings. This actually cleared up a lot of difficult parts of the Bible for me. God called Abraham who responded in faith, but never perfectly. When I actually read the whole story of Abraham for the first time, what struck me were all the times Abraham doubted or tried to do it his own way—repeatedly messing with God's plan. Finally we come to the story of God commanding Abraham to sacrifice Isaac his son. In obedience Abraham proceeds to do just that, and at the last minute God intervenes and provides a ram to sacrifice.

How could God command such an evil thing in the first place? In Deuteronomy 18:10, God specifically forbids the sacrifice of children and calls it detestable. The idea that God would command something so detestable and immoral, just to test Abraham, then intervene to stop him after he passed the test, hardly seems like God. Would God tell people to do something evil just to see if they would obey even an immoral and wicked command?

We might see this instead as one more example of Abraham's faltering faith. He moved ahead even when he couldn't hear clearly or see completely. God in his grace kept patiently intervening to put Abraham back on track. Abraham's heart was in the right place in wanting to follow wherever God led him. He just didn't always hear very clearly. Maybe the way Abraham heard God speaking wasn't really very different from the way you and I hear God speak when we are really trying to hear and obey God's voice. Even at its best, we often just sense what we believe God is saying. We don't actually hear an audible voice, but we do at times sense God's call or God's nudging. Then without the absolute knowledge we would like to have, we step out in faith straining to hear the next thing. We would all like to see a burning bush but seldom do.

Perhaps Abraham did hear a real audible voice. Maybe that was required to get him to make such a radical move away from his homeland and his people. But what if he heard God's call just like you and me? That would explain why after years passed, he began to doubt or second-guess what he thought God had promised. It would explain why he decided to have a son through Sarah's servant Hagar, since Sarah was obviously too old. It would explain why, if he saw other tribes in Canaan sacrificing their children to their gods, he may have wondered if he would be willing to make such a great sacrifice to his God. If he was determined to obey God whatever the cost, he may have convinced himself that God really was calling him to sacrifice his son. In any case we know that God intervened to save him from his own zeal, which is a pretty strong clue that it wasn't God's will for him in the first place.

Would it be safe to look at all Old Testament passages through the lens of Jesus to test if the God described sounded like the God Jesus knew? If God commands Israel to slay all the people of Jericho including women and children and cattle (Josh. 6:21), does that sound like the God of Jesus? Then maybe the writer of that story didn't get it right when he tells us what God wanted.

This is a pretty clear test and makes Jesus the central litmus test of all revelation. That squares with the centrality of Jesus as God's revealed Word. You'll have to decide if it squares with your idea of inspiration. I suggest because it rests on one standard—Jesus—it may be less arbitrary than making the whole Bible your standard. The Bible is so broad it can be made to support almost anything and indeed throughout history has been used to support slavery and polygamy and other outrageous evils and to promote hundreds of heretical cults. Apparently the Bible isn't the clear indisputable standard many claim or hope for. Believing the Bible is without any errors hasn't protected the church from error in the slightest.

THE DIALOGUE WITHIN THE BIBLE

We don't even need to go to Jesus in some cases to find a differing point of view. Within the Old Testament itself we find differing views if we allow ourselves to admit that possibility. For example, in several places God tells Israel to not mistreat the aliens in their midst for they were once aliens themselves (Exod. 22:21, 23:9). Then at other places prophets or leaders tell the people they must have nothing to do with foreigners in their midst, or they are to wipe out all the inhabitants in the land, or put away foreign wives they have taken (Ezra 10:10-12). Some might argue these differing commands were for different situations, while others believe there were differing opinions in Israel for how they should relate to those outside their ethnic community. All these differing opinions show up in the Bible stories.

A more significant difference may have to do with the importance of sacrifices. Exodus, Leviticus, and Numbers go into great detail about all the rituals for sacrifices—all of which God has commanded and specified. Then the prophets came along and said, "Do you think God desires sacrifices? No he wants an obedient heart." Or "I'll tell you the sacrifice God wants. He wants a contrite heart and justice and mercy" (my paraphrases of Isa. 1:11-17, Amos 5:21-24, Hosea 6:6, Ps. 40:6 and 51:16-17).

Again, maybe the prophets were just saying the sacrifices were meaningless if they were just empty ritual not backed up with true repentance. But Jeremiah says,

> When I brought your ancestors out of Egypt and spoke to them, I did not give them commands about burnt offerings and sacrifices, but I gave them this command: Obey me and I will be your God and you will be my people. (Jer. 7:21-23)

Maybe the prophets actually thought that the organized, ritualized religion of the temple was meaningless to God's real concerns and God didn't want sacrifices at all. That would fit with our own experience of diverse opinions within the church community—those who support organized religion and those who think something more spontaneous and less structured is more authentic.

In the New Testament we see there were disagreements in the early church. The book of Acts tells of a conference in Jerusalem to iron out these disagreements. We still see some of the differences between those with more Jewish concerns like the book of James and Matthew's Gospel and those more open to having less Jewish influence for the sake of the wider Gentile church like John's gospel and epistles and Paul's letters. I admit these differences are much more nuanced and need much more teasing out than the Old Testament dialogue between the viewpoints of king, priest, and prophet.

These aren't things I have definite settled opinions about except that I'm open to considering the possibility of different voices within the Scripture carrying on an open conversation or even a debate about what God and faith are about. If you just can't allow for these differences within Scripture, I don't need to argue you out of that—as long as you don't then settle on a belief you think is biblical that doesn't rest on loving God with all your heart and your neighbor as yourself. In other words if you don't ignore Jesus because you choose to believe something in Leviticus that is more practical or suits you better.

I'm comfortable with Christians who read every word of Scripture literally including what Jesus says. Even if you believe some things are a lot more literal than I do, I don't have any need to talk you out of your belief or straighten you out. If Jesus is central to how you believe and live, you are my sisters and brothers (if you will have me).

Chapter Ten

GRACE AND FORGIVENESS

The Pharisees were bothered by the forgiveness and friendship Jesus extended to sinners. They were always concerned about other people's morals. Lots of people didn't live up to the Pharisees' standards, which they based on their study of Scripture. They were sure they were right. So they judged many people as sinners and included Jesus because he ate with sinners. The Pharisees accused Jesus of drinking too much wine and partying with low-lifes—*and* the Gospels don't refute the charge.

What would we think today of someone who did what Jesus did then? Jesus is at a wedding reception where the guests have already drunk all the wine. His mother comes and asks him to take care of the problem. So he produces three more huge jars of wine to enable the wedding celebration and the drinking to go on.

This reminds me of the joke Ronald Reagan told of the Baptist who was offered a drink and said, "Oh no, I never touch the stuff." The person who offered said, "But even Jesus drank wine."

To which the good Baptist replied, "Yes, but I'd think more of him if he hadn't."

WHO ARE THE "PROSTITUTES AND SINNERS" TODAY?

What are we to make of the "prostitutes and sinners" Jesus was repeatedly accused of hanging out with? This makes me ask how many prostitutes are flocking around Jesus' followers now. Few Christian churches are attracting prostitutes today. They would be uncomfortable around most of us Christians. Somehow the people looked down on by the rest of Jesus' society felt comfortable around Jesus.

His reputation for hanging with the wrong crowd makes me wonder: If he were here today, might he have a serious gay and lesbian following? I know, every time the Bible mentions same-gender relations these are condemned, but I also know Jesus never discussed it. Jesus actually seldom addressed sexual sins. He did address divorce at various places and equated lust with adultery (Matt. 5:27-28).

The Scripture clearly said that adulterers should be stoned. Yet Jesus felt no need to carry out what the Scripture commanded. He did tell the woman caught in the act of adultery to go and leave her life of sin, but the first thing he said to her was that he wasn't going to condemn her either (John 8:1-11).

I find myself pulled in a lot of directions regarding homosexuality. I end up being pretty sure I want to err on the side of grace rather than erring on the side of judgment.

Thirty to fifty years ago the big issue in the church was divorce and whether divorced people could be allowed to stay in the church as members in good standing. Wouldn't the church just be condoning divorce? And Jesus did say something about that—he was against it pretty strongly. Then a lot of families in the church began to have daughters and sons and sisters or uncles who were going through the agony of divorce; those families realized that if ever their children needed the church, it was at a difficult time like this. Somehow most of us changed and divorced people remained in the church without the church having to promote or condone divorce as a good thing. We even got better at not making divorced people feel condemned or like failures.

During that time my wife's church was struggling with whether they could allow a divorced and remarried couple to join their church. A woman in the church told my wife and me that all she knew was that when she was standing before the judgment throne she was a lot more worried that God would tell her she had been too judgmental than that she hadn't been judgmental enough. That has always stuck with me.

The sticking point on the divorce question for a lot of churches was whether the church could allow remarriage for divorced people. Again much of the evangelical church just couldn't find the heart to say that once someone's marriage had failed, they then had to remain single the rest of their life. I don't think this was so much a thought-out theological or scriptural decision as a realization that love and compassion required openness and grace be extended to each person to do what they felt God was leading them to.

TODAY IT'S MEMBERS OF THE LGBT COMMUNITY

Once again families and friends and churches with sons and daughters who identify as LGBT (lesbian, gay, bisexual, transgendered) are struggling with how to be true to their faith and still support and love a member of their family. For some that means full acceptance of their sexuality, for others the question is how to love a person who identifies as LGBT when they believe they can't accept same-gender relations. Not only are the church and the families struggling to come to grips with this but Christians who are themselves LGBT have differing beliefs. Some persons who identify as LGBT are much more comfortable affirming this than others are. Many struggle greatly with their own sexuality.

The tragedy is that some are so distraught over their sexuality and their inability to overcome their feelings that they despair and commit suicide. Something is seriously wrong if the church's message creates an atmosphere that leads to such despair. There needs to be a greater note of grace for persons who identify as LGBT and not only if they can remain celibate. The suicide rates among persons who are LGBT is too high. This also strongly suggests that identifying as LGBT is not simply a choice. Who would deliberately choose such a life of being ostracized and ridiculed?

Although I lean toward offering much grace in this area, I'm not always sure how Christians should respond. I understand why many churches are reluctant to accept simply normalizing LGBT relationships within the church community. Something within many of us holds back; sometimes this is the common and often problematic human aversion to whatever is not considered "normal" in a given community. However, this also often has everything to do with accepting the Bible as a norm for how we are called to live without always changing our morals right along with our ever-changing culture.

So I am neither entirely comfortable with complete acceptance of LGBT relationships nor with a position of opposition to LGBT relationships within the church. Being in that in-between state I can only respond with a great deal of sensitivity, caring, and love for the people I know who identify as LGBT. I can't imagine Jesus responding in any other way. My friends who are LGBT are themselves some of the best examples I know of the Christ-like qualities of caring and love.

I read the book *UnChristian* by David Kinnaman and Gabe Lyons. The book is about the terribly negative way *non*-Christian people view Christians. Christians are widely seen, especially by those in their twenties and thirties, as judgmental, hypocritical, homophobic, and too political. Although the authors take a conservative stance toward homosexual practice, they call for much more love and friendship to be shown to persons who identify as LGBT. They believe Christians have singled out this one issue as a far greater sin than all the other "normal" sins.

In Romans 1, Paul lumps same-gender sexual expression in with greed, slander, and all the other sins we tolerate in the church all the time. In fact as they point out, the church and our own lives are filled with other kinds of sexual brokenness for which we all need God's grace.

I understand why churches are responding in different ways to such a difficult question. I understand churches that expect a different standard of behavior within the church community than in the surrounding culture. The purpose of those standards isn't simply to control other people but to promote a life of fullness and openness before God and within the church community.

I also understand churches that decide to love and accept gay people without judgment. My prayer for gays in the church is to see their relationship with God grow as God works in their lives in the same way God works in my life despite my own fallen nature. I don't believe either position reflects an unwillingness to take the Bible seriously. Both churches are struggling to find the most loving and faithful way to deal with a difficult issue. I believe we also need to show a lot more love and grace toward *churches* that are ministering to gay persons in a different way than we are.

Our experience with gay relationships clearly shows the difficulty (or near impossibility) of people overcoming or even controlling their same-sex attraction—even among prominent and respected government and church leaders. Even the most conservative Christians should be able to see that apart from a relationship with Christ and a structure of accountability, no one can control same-sex attractions or live a celibate life. Many would argue that can't happen even *with* a strong Christian commitment. So why the huge movement to oppose gay marriage, or even civil unions, as a matter of public policy in the secular society?

If persons who are LGBT in a secular society are not going to change their attractions and relationships, then celibacy is hardly an option for most LGBT people outside the church community. Do we really want to promote a promiscuous life of one-night stands over a committed, loving relationship to one partner? Even for public health reasons, the latter has to be far healthier for persons who are straight or LGBT—not to mention what it does for one's emotional health and self-respect.

I understand some will trot out statistics that show true monogamy is rarer in LGBT relationships than in straight ones, but that's hardly an argument against *promoting* monogamy as a better public policy. A hard-nosed stance in opposition to open, loving, committed LGBT relationships is hardly going to keep more people from being LGBT, and it certainly won't make LGBT people think the church has their best interests at heart. They will inevitably feel the church condemns them, and they will have nothing to do with such close-minded people. Promoting monogamous same-gender relationships in civil society is not going to turn more people LGBT. And why do we want to use secular law to enforce or promote religious beliefs in the first place?

Hard-nosed condemnation of all LGBT relationships in secular society opens the church, as we have seen, to the charge of hypocrisy for setting a standard of abstinence that many within the church, including some church leaders, have not been able to live up to. Jesus said, "Woe to you religious experts, because you load people down with burdens you can hardly carry, and you yourselves will hardly lift a finger to help them" (Luke 11:46, and Matt. 23:2-4).

PRACTICING WHAT WE PREACH

It's certainly true that anyone struggling with temptation should show a lot of grace and forgiveness to others struggling with the same issues. When a religious leader who has loudly opposed LGBT relationships is discovered to have been involved in a gay relationship, we immediately hear charges of hypocrisy. While that is understandable, I'm not sure the charge of hypocrisy is always fair.

The secular assumption is that preaching against something, then falling for the same temptation is hypocritical. I think hypocrisy is being hard on the sins of others but easy on your own. Hypocrisy is judging others, and justifying yourself. But we all, to one extent or another, fail to live up to our own ideals and standards whether we are Christians or not. We all find that our friends disappoint us and that we disappoint ourselves. This should make us all less judgmental and more forgiving of the failings of others.

Jesus' harshest words—his words of condemnation and judgment—weren't leveled against "sinners" but against the religious folks who stood in judgment over them. Jesus levels the field by saying that those who look with lust have committed adultery already. Those who hate are on a par with murderers. So we all stand as sinners in need of grace. We are all broken and hardly in a position to condemn anyone. We should all be extending a lot more grace and forgiveness than we do. Over and over Jesus forgave almost unilaterally it seems. To each of us Jesus says simply, "Go and sin no more."

Like Jesus, we need to be a forgiving people, because we ourselves so often need forgiveness, both for when we screw up but also sometimes for just being ourselves. Because just being ourselves can at times require a good deal of forgiveness from others.

Jesus taught God's forgiveness of us requires our forgiveness of others. He even said this in the Lord's Prayer—"Forgive us our sins as we forgive those who sin against us."

Jesus says clearly that unforgiveness is the unforgivable sin. If you don't forgive others, God won't forgive you (Matt. 6:15). We pretty much take God's grace and forgiveness for granted. If we confess our sins, God will forgive us, right? But Jesus says God *won't*, if we don't forgive others their sins. It sounds like God is saying, "Don't come looking for grace from me if you aren't willing to offer grace to others for their offenses" (Matt. 18:23-35). That is pretty sobering.

BREAKFAST WITH A PROSTITUTE

I started this chapter telling how prostitutes were among Jesus' followers, but few prostitutes are coming into churches today. If we have no contact, how can we offer God's grace and acceptance and forgiveness?

A few years ago I was pastoring a small church near downtown San Antonio. One morning I went to the Home Depot to pick up some things to do some repairs at the church. On the way back I decided to stop and get some breakfast at Pepe's, a small Mexican restaurant. I think they had the cheapest breakfast in San Antonio—huevos rancheros (two eggs with salsa on them) with refried beans, potatoes, and tortillas for $1.29, or you could have the same thing with a pork chop for $1.95. For those prices I had breakfast there often.

So as I was heading for the restaurant around eleven o'-clock, I went down a street where there were frequently girls walking the street looking for business. At a stop light this girl looked at me with this question on her face as if to ask if I were interested. I shook my head and smiled and drove on up the street. But it bothered me because she didn't have the hardened look of most of the prostitutes I'd seen before. She just looked like any other decent young woman—fresh-faced and smiling. I wondered what she would have said if I had offered to take her along for breakfast, but that seemed pretty far out, so I kept driving for another dozen blocks to the restaurant. Yet the idea wouldn't let go of me. I decided to go back. If she was still there, I would ask her and see what she said. I thought she would probably turn me down.

I had no idea what I would say if she agreed, but I did pray for some guidance. When I got back to the corner she was still there. I pulled up to the stop light again and rolled down my window as she walked over. I asked if she would let me buy her some breakfast. She asked what I would pay her, and I said, "Nothing, I just want to have breakfast with you." She said "Okay" and got in.

We drove for a little while. I asked, "Aren't you scared doing this? You never know who's picking you up."

She said, "Sometimes." Then she told me about a recent guy who had picked her up and started getting pretty rough, but she had managed to get away.

I asked why she kept doing something so dangerous, and she told me it was the only way she could pay for her drugs—crack.

I asked if she ever thought about quitting and she said, yes, but she couldn't yet because she really didn't want to stop doing crack just yet. But, she added, she knew she could quit if she wanted, she just wasn't ready.

We got to the restaurant and ordered breakfast. Over breakfast I asked, "Do you have any kids?"

"Two—a little boy and a girl. They're with my grand-mother."

"What about your mother?' I asked, and she told me her mom was on the street too, but she was in a lot worse shape because she was doing heroin and had been for years. I just kind of groaned inside.

When I asked, "Don't you miss your kids?" she turned very quiet and got tears in her eyes. "I haven't seen them for six months."

"Why?" I asked.

"It's just too hard. Every time I go to my grandma's, my kids want me to stay, and I just can't."

"That really hurts you, doesn't it?" I asked and she nodded.

She went on to tell me that she and her husband had both had good jobs, but she was doing crack with one of her girlfriends, and her husband didn't know. She caught her husband with another woman and threw him out. Then she couldn't make ends meet, her kids stayed more and more with her grandma. She kept doing more crack and finally had to start prostituting herself to support her habit.

I asked if she ever prayed. She did sometimes. I told her I would pray that she would be able to get back to her kids and have the strength to walk away from what she was doing because it was killing her.

She said, "I know."

I told her there were lots of people who would care about her and her kids and give her lots of friendship and support, and I could help her hook up with people like that. Then I got scared because I wasn't at all sure the women in my church whom I had in mind would really do that.

I asked if I could pray with her and she said okay. So I did.

Then I took her back to her corner and dropped her off. I saw her again a few weeks later and asked if she wanted lunch, so she went with me again. She told me she had gone back to see her kids and stayed for three days, but then she had had to leave. She didn't think she could go back anytime soon. It was just too difficult for her kids when she left. We talked over lunch. I asked if she wanted me to pray with her again and she did. She had tears in her eyes.

After that I only saw her once, and she said she couldn't go with me. That was the last I saw her. I felt God had put me in her life for some reason, even if I had no idea whether anything had come of my visits. Maybe a seed was planted. The whole thing broke my heart.

She was really a sweet girl and was just destroying herself and her kids as well. If I had any fantasies before about prostitutes being exotic and kind of brazen, or having a blatant sexuality, I certainly saw something else when seeing and speaking to her face to face. I saw instead a person who was transparent and vulnerable—not needing to put on any front since I already knew what she was. She seemed like a person who saw little hope or future.

I think prostitutes followed Jesus because he offered forgiveness without condemnation. He also offered hope. I understood the forgiveness Jesus extended to the broken people who followed after him. I really wished Jesus' followers were more invested in that kind of forgiveness and ministry.

Chapter Eleven

JESUS' "I HAVE A DREAM" SPEECH

Jesus came preaching good news. If we take what he said honestly, without reading back into it our theologies of salvation, many of which developed in the early church in the years after Jesus' death, he talked almost exclusively about people accepting God's love and forgiveness, changing their old ways of thinking, and living in a new way centered on love for God and neighbor. He referred to this new life as entering into God's reign.

The early believers were called followers of the Way. That's what Jesus meant when he told Nicodemus we must be reborn or "born again" to enter God's reign. Actually his first statement was that no one could *see* God's reign without being reborn or born from above (John 3:3). Was he suggesting we couldn't *recognize* God's reign without new eyes?

The good news Jesus preached was that if the people of Israel really started living the way he called them to live, they would be freed from worries and doubts. The poor would have enough. The sick would be taken care of. Slaves would be freed. Debts would be forgiven. Class differences would disappear. They would live in peace with the Romans. In short, *shalom* would break out, which is exactly what was to happen when the Messiah came.

The problem, as you can see looking at the list, is that none of them expected the Messiah's coming to cost *them* anything. They expected it to just happen and they would gain something. They all wanted the shalom of God to break out in Israel but not at the expense of their own agendas or interests. Everybody awaited the year of Jubilee—the *"acceptable year of the Lord"* as Isaiah says (Isa. 61:1-2). They awaited its being proclaimed, *sometime*, because that was the year all debts were canceled and all slaves freed and all land went back to the original families who had owned it. It was a year of economic and social leveling supposed to come every fifty years in Israel (Lev. 25:8ff). We have no story in the Bible or anywhere else to indicate that it ever actually occurred or was practiced even once.

But Jesus proclaimed the year of Jubilee had come when he used the Isaiah passage as his inaugural address:

> The Spirit of the Lord is on me, because he has anointed me to proclaim good news to the poor. He has sent me to proclaim freedom for the prisoners and recovery of sight for the blind, to set the oppressed free, to proclaim the year of the Lord's favor.

His audience probably knew this passage from Isaiah 61 by heart, and Jesus left out the last line which was probably their favorite part, *"and the day of vengeance of our God."* They were astonished at his words of grace (Luke 4:14-21).

Jesus went on to say he wasn't going to do any of the miracles in his home town like he had done in Capernaum, a Gentile town. Then as if to rub in the point he gave other examples of God's grace toward Gentiles, the widow who fed Elijah and Naaman healed by Elisha, while overlooking all the widows and lepers in Israel. They were furious at this suggestion that God might pass them over and bless non-Jews or Gentiles instead. They were ready to throw Jesus from a cliff, but he slipped away.

Besides in this inaugural sermon, Jesus called for many other changes in people's hearts and lives. The problem was, no one wanted actually to forgive the debts people owed them. And how could anyone afford to just free slaves? Who would do the work? No one wanted to give hard-earned money to poor folks who would just waste it. The upper-class folks didn't really want the walls to be erased. They didn't want to be best friends with the lower class or those with "no class" at all. And they sure didn't want to start loving the Romans who were oppressing them. They could hardly wait until the Messiah came and crushed the pagan Romans.

The irony, if you think about it, is that none of that would have killed them. I can still hear my mother saying, "It's not going to kill you," when she was asking us to do something we didn't want to do. But whether we are speaking figuratively, like she was, or literally, if Israel had followed what Jesus taught, it wouldn't have *killed* them. But it seems they would rather have died than agree to what Jesus was calling them to do and be.

In contrast, if Jesus had started a revolution as everyone expected the Messiah to do, I'm sure thousands of young Jews would have gladly joined a revolution against Rome. Parents would have proudly sacrificed their sons to the battle for the nation. So they would have *literally* rather died, and offered their children to die, than do what Jesus called them to do—to give up their worries, their status, the debts owed them, the slaves they owned, wealth and land they had accumulated, their moral superiority, their despising of sinners and tax collectors, their exclusion of Gentiles and Samaritans, and especially their hatred for the Romans,

We can see why the poor, the outcasts, and the sinners followed Jesus and embraced his message; they didn't have a lot to lose. In contrast, the well-off, the religious scholars and members of the establishment, mostly stayed away and had lots of doubts about Jesus. But you just can't read Jesus honestly without seeing he really wanted people to live by different religious, social, and economic priorities. The heart of worship or religion to him was compassion, not the rules of the Law.

Jesus talked about money all the time. Jesus really expected people to live by different social rules and break down class walls and ethnic hatreds and prejudices. He said don't just invite your friends over or those who can invite you back, invite people outside your social circle. Jesus really wanted people to be much more forgiving and accepting of both brothers and sisters and of outsiders and strangers. He called on people to break down walls as he did.

Remember the Samaritan woman he struck up a conversation with at the well? She was so surprised that he would speak to her that she responded, "Excuse me? How is it you, a Jewish man, are speaking to me, a Samaritan woman?" It just wasn't done. I wonder if she thought at first that maybe he was trying to hit on her.

Jesus really wanted the people of Israel to respond with love toward the Romans. If forced to carry a Roman soldier's bag for a mile, carry it two (Matt. 5:41). He asked them to stop hating their Roman enemy and even suggested praying for them (v. 44). That would have been a real stretch!

Jesus may simply have been calling Israel to be pragmatic because the path of provocation the Zealots were taking was suicidal and would lead to the destruction of Israel. Jesus wept over Jerusalem saying, "If only you had known what would bring you peace" (Luke 19:41-44). Jesus went on to predict the resulting calamity which actually happened in 70 CE. If they *had* heeded Jesus and given up their hatred of the Romans and their armed insurrection, the Romans would not have destroyed the temple and driven the Jews out of Jerusalem. When the Roman empire fell several hundred years later, the Jews would have still been in Jerusalem instead of scattered all across the Mediterranean world. Yet they probably thought Jesus was naïve and idealistic!

But Jesus wasn't just being pragmatic. He also called them to love the Romans who persecuted them, as an example of God's love because God loves indiscriminately *and so that we may be our Father's children* (Matt. 5:44-47). He called the peacemakers, "blessed" and said they would be called children of God (Matt. 5:9). If you want to be like your Daddy, love your enemies, because he loves them. How could you possibly persuade them of their parent's love for them by trying to destroy them?

THE KINGDOM OF GOD WAS JESUS' DREAM

Jesus had a dream that one day Israel would be a light to all nations and that all the people of the earth would be blessed through her. The people of Israel were chosen by God not because they were his favorites but with an awesome calling to demonstrate to the world how God's people are to live. Words on tablets can only go so far. But words lived out in the life of a person, or the life of a community, are far more powerful. We see that in the incarnation, God came to us in the flesh—the living Word. Jesus wanted to expand the life of God lived out in the life of a community. He referred to it as the reign or kingdom of God. He talked about it all the time. The kingdom of God was his dream for the world, spreading from Israel to all nations. From his inaugural address on, Jesus declared his dream a reality: "Today this Scripture is fulfilled" (Luke 4:21).

Jesus saw the reign of God as entailing not a new set of rules or laws but a new mindset. Jesus approached life with the full confidence that God loves us and can be trusted to have our best interests at heart. Jesus spells out not with creeds or theological formulations but with stories this new way of looking at the world and this new way of understanding God. If you get the story, you will have a pretty good idea what God is like and what God wants for us and for the world.

Jesus' agenda was the salvation of Israel and ultimately the world. He was interested in saving the whole lot (John 3:16), not just Israel or a few individuals. He certainly called and ministered to individuals, but with the intention of getting them to join in God's reign, which he was inaugurating, whereby the world would be saved. His prayer was that "God's kingdom come and God's will be done on earth as in heaven." Jesus taught and demonstrated how God made the world to work. He had the owner's manual. He in effect *was* the first "interactive" owner's manual—the Word in flesh. God's world would only work when people got the big picture and dedicated their lives to that picture, the reign of God. If people could just see this big picture, they might be less concerned about their own self-interests and care more about the whole community. So it was a costly challenge and an awesome calling.

We often talk of salvation as being totally free. True, we can never *earn* God's grace and forgiveness. But Jesus never talked about a free, no-obligation offer. He told people to be sure they counted the cost before they joined in following him (Luke 14:28-33). He didn't want a bunch of people to join only to leave when it got tough. He talked about things like a pearl of such great value that a merchant sold everything he had because he just *had* to have that pearl (Matt. 13:45-46). That is how Jesus described the great prize he was offering people—to join in the kingdom of heaven. But he never suggested it was free. He said it would cost us everything.

THE "BE ATTITUDES"

Jesus didn't primarily spell out laws; he told stories that showed the attitude we need to have. Even where Jesus spells out in one long sermon how we should live, it seems to be more about a way of seeing and being than a list of "Thou-shalt-not's." His Sermon on the Mount is his "I have a dream" speech (Matt. 5-7). In God's kingdom, he begins, the tables are turned. Those who the rest of world think must be cursed are here blessed. He gives a long list of those who are blessed in the new order of God's reign.

The poor in spirit are blessed for the kingdom belongs to them. Luke's version just says, "Blessed are the poor." Did Jesus say it two different ways? Or did each writer use a different spin? Matthew's seems more spiritualized and Luke's more down to earth. Luke's list of those who are blessed has a list of counterpoint woes (Luke 6: 24-26). "Woe to you who are rich, for you have already received your comfort." If Jesus said the Beatitudes once, and Matthew and Luke recorded them differently, then Luke's version is probably closer to the original because of this counterpoint, which would make no sense alongside the "poor in spirit." Some scholars think Jesus said it both ways in different situations.

"Poor in spirit," always seemed to me quite different than to be literally poor. But they aren't so far apart if interpreted as Thomas Stobie does in an article I read online. His understanding is that "poor in spirit" is an attitude of how we attach ourselves to our possessions. It is not so much to take a vow of poverty as to adopt a spirit of poverty, holding nothing we have more valuable than the kingdom of God. With this interpretation both writers are referring to poverty or an attitude of poverty, rather than a spiritual condition. This fits with Jesus' call to forsake all to follow him and aligns us with the poor. Even those of us with plenty are called to identify with the poor—counting them as our sisters and brothers.

I've worked with poor folks most of my life. I have often had volunteers come to work in the poor communities where I've been. Often they will say something like, "I never realized just how blessed I am." They mean all their nice stuff and the privileges they have. It's great that they are faced with the huge disparity between how they live and how much of the rest of the world lives. But Jesus suggests their "blessings" may be a reason for sorrow, and in the end the poor person will be the blessed one. Some Christian writers (see Appendix I) don't want to read that understanding into what Jesus says, but "Woe to you who are rich . . . " almost necessarily pulls us to that interpretation.

Jesus goes on to call blessed those who are meek, because as Psalm 37 says, they will inherit the earth but their oppressors will be no more. This and other Beatitudes tell us that the tables will be turned; one day those who mourn will be comforted (Luke says they will laugh), those who are hungry will be fed (Luke 6:21), or those who hunger for justice will be satisfied. Others will be rewarded. The merciful will be shown mercy. The pure in heart will see God. The peacemakers will be called God's children. Those who are persecuted for being righteous—the kingdom of God is theirs. Blessed are those who are insulted, persecuted, and lied about because the prophets have always been treated like that. Luke adds, "Woe to you when everyone speaks well of you, for that is how their ancestors treated the false prophets" (Luke 6:26).

Why does Jesus start out by telling us all this misery will become a good thing? I think he wants to take the way we think and how we see the world and turn it upside down. Jesus completely turns the tables on what the Pharisees taught and the kind of people they were. As Luke points out, Jesus' good news to the poor is sometimes necessarily bad news for the rich.

What does God think when he sees the huge disparity between those who have plenty and others who have so little and are starving? Clearly it's a problem to God. It demonstrates that his world isn't working the way God intended. The problem is our lack of compassion and our unwillingness to feel any responsibility for the beat-up and robbed guy in the ditch. After all, we didn't put him there. Jesus says the real neighbor is the kind and generous gay man who stops to take care of the guy and even pays out of his own pocket while good church folks walked on by. I think gay is probably a pretty good substitute for "Samaritans" in our day (Luke 10:25-37).

Jesus has a dream of a community of God that is like a shining city on a hill. Like a burning lamp that can't be hidden under a basket. I heard a preacher who said, "You may be able to cover up the flame with a bushel basket for a little while, but if the lamp burns bright enough it will soon set the whole basket on fire and then the light will really be bright!"

Jesus calls us to obey the whole law, but he isn't after the letter of the law. His concern is the spirit in which God made the law in the first place. Jesus assumes the whole law rests on the twin mandates to love God with everything we have and to love our neighbor as ourselves. In that light he speaks of murder and hatred being the same sin, as is adultery and lust. He says the law may allow divorce, but that isn't God's vision for marriage.

He calls for us to be honest without having to embellish. I often hear people telling me about something and then saying, "Well I'm going to tell you the truth . . . " as though they hadn't been up to that point. Or people who say something and then add, "and that's the truth," which really makes me wonder, since they had to say that.

Then Jesus gives some really counter-intuitive advice about not defending yourself when you are struck or sued, or forced into service, and even suggests we offer the other person the opportunity to do it again. The first time you may be the victim, but the second time you *offered* to take it. There is something disarming about a surprise move like that. There is real power in this disarming strategy. Most of all it seems like the way of Jesus. He calls us to treat enemies as friends, because he says God does. Our love is to be perfect, unconditional, and unadulterated like God's love is. If the purpose of all our relationships is to free others from their bondage to the "dark side," what else would redeem that other person intent on dominating you? If the insult ends after falling on us and isn't returned, we have absorbed the violence.

Jesus had a dream of spiritual followers who would fast and pray and give alms. They would do all this for God's sake and not to be noticed or for show, so people would think well of them.

He saw a world in which people would give freely whatever they had without need to hoard or keep back what someone else seriously needed. A world where people wouldn't then worry about their own needs—which is of course why we save and horde and don't give freely to others, because we *do* worry about what would happen to us. Jesus doesn't say, Don't *plan* for tomorrow. Instead he says, Don't *worry* about tomorrow. And don't hoard things. I think Americans will always need to struggle with that. I have to struggle with it, because our culture assures us we need to put aside a lot to survive. At another place Jesus tells us it is hard for rich folks to enter into God's reign, so I suppose most of us Americans will struggle with all of Jesus' challenges about money.

Jesus saw a world in which his followers would not judge others, realizing they had enough faults of their own to keep them busy. He called us to trust in God absolutely, to simply ask and seek and knock if we need anything. God is ready to answer our call.

SECRETS OF THE KINGDOM

Besides this incredible speech that lays out Jesus' dream of how we could live together if only we trusted our loving divine parent and weren't so afraid of death, Jesus told many more stories to illustrate not the letter but the spirit of God's will for us, God's children. Jesus unfolded the secrets of the reign of God—secrets of the universe actually. He unfolded the counter-intuitive way the world is made to run.

Jesus calls the dark force that rules our world the ruler of this age. Our own fears of death tell us we have to look out for ourselves first of all. Kill or be killed. Don't let anyone take advantage or get the better of you.

Jesus tells us to keep our eyes on the needs of others and not worry about ourselves. Be ruled by compassion for all we encounter, because they are all deeply loved by God. Even those who want to harm us are to be won back from the dark side, so don't worry about losing *to* them. Worry about losing *them* to the darkness, or the darkness will overtake us as well.

Through many other stories and miracles of healing and restoration Jesus taught and demonstrated the love and care of a loving, healing, forgiving, restoring God he called "*Abba*." Although the life Jesus calls us to seems nearly impossible, he assures us that like any parent who loves their child, God loves us so much more than we ever could and wants the very best for us.

We resist this message of life because we fear the cost to our loved ones and ourselves. Yet we sell out so easily to the deception of this age and the fleeting kingdoms and powers of this age who ask for the sacrifice of even the sons and daughters we love and hold so dear. Getting tough with our enemies seems so much more realistic than loving them. Thus we are seduced by the power of death and sin. Remember what I said earlier, that most sin is ultimately tied to our fear of death? And, we might add, our willingness to employ the means of death to save ourselves from what we fear so much.

CAPTIVATED BY DEATH

Jesus repudiated the deception that only violence can save us—that violence is the only realistic response to human evil. Despite being with Jesus for three years, his disciples could not wrap their heads around the idea of defeating evil by accepting death on a cross. Jesus rejected kill or be killed; he accepted death from his enemies. We understand that in Jesus' case, his death was to save the world including his enemies. We often fail to understand that the cross Jesus calls us to also embrace makes just as much sense as the cross he accepted.

Let me give a current example. In the midst of the post-9-11 Iraq war, a Christian Peacemaker Team was in Iraq during some of the most dangerous times. They weren't in the "green zone" protected by the military but out in the neighborhoods of Baghdad working to bring reconciliation and understanding among different factions, between Iraqi citizens and insurgents and the military. Many thought the CPTers were naïve idealists not facing the hard realities of how evil the insurgents were. The CPT members actually were well aware that what they were doing was very dangerous, but they chose to stay.

After working there for many months, four men were kidnapped and held for weeks. Finally one of the members of the team was killed and soon after that the rest were freed by a military raid. Some commentators said this showed how naïve the CPTers were. They saw the death of this one man as a "reality check" for those who thought this could be an effective means of ending violence. The fact that thousands had already died for the violent option and the country was still filled with violence wasn't seen as naïve at all.

That is what I mean when I say we are enamored with violence and death, thinking it alone will save us. So we look to the ways of death to *save* us from death. We offer our sons and daughters and spouses to die to save ourselves and keep our families "safe." It has ever been thus.

SALVATION—SAVED FROM DEATH

The story of humanity's salvation is that while we were still God's enemies Christ died because of our sin and alienation from God. God created everything good, but the forces of sin and death and violence took over the world by deception, posing as our savior. Fearing death, humanity bought the deception, and allowed death to rule us. God tried in many ways to win us back from the allure of our affair with death and violence, but even while we gave lip service to our devotion to God, humanity's wars and violence continued, we still lived by death's rules of greed and violence, thereby serving death.

Finally God saw that all his attempts to win his people back through emissaries or prophets and written instructions or law were not enough to turn our hearts. So God came to us in Christ, and lived among us, sharing our flesh and our limitations. Though he shared our limitations, the forces of evil did not stifle the force of life and the light he was. He embodied light and shone into all our dark places and fears. He called us to the light, and was himself the light. But we, in our blindness and fear of death, did not recognize that God had come to us to call us to the light.

Because we had a distorted view of God we did not recognize him when he walked among us. We took him for an imposter—a blasphemer. To protect our image of God, distorted by our allegiance to the forces of death, we had him killed. We killed the very source of light and life when he was in our midst, because his light challenged the darkness that we thought was truth and light. We were so captivated by sin and death we feared light and judged it as wrong. Thus Jesus died for our sins, actually as a direct result of our greatest sin. Our own alienation from God drove us to kill him. There could be no greater sin or miscarriage of justice than to kill the very source of light, mistaking it for darkness.

Having silenced or killed all the prophets who came before, we now killed God's anointed one, Emanuel—God with us. I say "we" to include ourselves directly in this, because we still largely silence the voice of the prophets and of Jesus in our own world, our churches, and in our own lives.

Death defeated

God could have responded to such an injustice and rejection by wiping us out for all our sin and rebellion and our allegiance to death. Instead God in his mercy reversed Jesus' death sentence and brought back to life the Light *we* had destroyed. God undid the injustice of our actions and undid the work of death. Rather than inflicting vengeance on us who put Christ to death, God forgave our participation in sin and death and thus opened the way for us back to him.

Jesus' was obedient even to the point of death, and God raised him back to life, thereby defeating death and saving us from death as well. By his death and resurrection our relationship to God is restored.

So if we now declare Jesus as the "Lord" of our life and get it into our heart that God actually raised him from the dead, we will be saved (Rom. 10:9). We are now free to turn from our darkness and from death, which God defeated, and toward the source of all light. We therefore are no longer in fear nor enamored by death and the ways of death. We know that there is no salvation, either in this world or the next, through death and all its deceptions. We therefore no longer serve death, because we are children of the light that lights up the world.

We are now called to be bearers of the light, no longer fearing anything death can do to us because death has been conquered by the light. We are called to the task of bearing the light to a dying world, still darkened by death and enamored by the ways of death. Our ministry is to call people away from their fear and their allegiance to death and the ways of death, recognizing that, as we once were, the people of this age are captives of death who need to be freed—saved, redeemed from death's allure. Therefore, if anyone is in Christ, it's a whole new world.

Remember when Jesus nearly got thrown from a cliff because he suggested God's grace extended to outsiders—non-Jews? The miracle of the church was indeed a new creation. It opened up a whole new world with Jews and non-Jews worshipping and eating together as the reconciled community of believers. The old has gone, the new has come. God was reconciling the world to himself in Christ and has given us also the ministry of reconciliation. So we are Christ's ambassadors as though God was making his appeal directly through us, Be reconciled (2 Cor. 5: 17-20)!

Like the One who went before us, we too may face death, because those whose allegiance is to death fear the light. They are not the foe but are ensnared by the foe. Our task is not to destroy them but to win them back to the light and to God, just as we have been won by Christ—the light of the world. We call all people and all rulers and all nations to forsake the dark forces and the ways of death and to live in the light of God, which is the only hope for the world. As followers of the slain Lamb, we live toward and await that day when we all can shout, "The kingdom of the world has become the kingdom of our Lord and of his Messiah, and he will reign forever and ever" (Rev. 11:15).

APPENDIX 1

Dallas Willard in his book *The Divine Conspiracy* pretty much glosses over Luke's sermon on the plain which says, "Blessed are the poor." Willard emphasizes instead Matthew's "the poor in spirit," which he translates as the spiritually impoverished or spiritual zeroes. Then he says Jesus is telling us the kingdom of heaven is nearby even for these spiritual midgets. Well, maybe, but I've never heard that take before. Willard is consistent with that interpretation and goes on to paint each of those whom Jesus says are blessed as actually embodying a negative aspect which God accepts and blesses anyway in God's grace. So, Willard says, none of the Beatitudes are aspects we should seek to practice in our own lives.

I just don't find that it makes sense to view peacemakers, the pure in heart, those who hunger for justice, the merciful, or those persecuted because they are righteous as embodying negative things. These seem more than problematic characteristics God accepts through grace.

I agree we shouldn't *seek* persecution. But Jesus is pretty clear that those who are persecuted are blessed in God's reign. I don't think it follows that neither should we seek to be peacemakers, or pure in heart, or merciful, or meek. Psalm 37, which Jesus must have been quoting from, also says that the meek will inherit the earth. "Wait patiently on the Lord, don't fret . . . A little while longer and the wicked will be no more, but the meek will inherit the earth." It's pretty clear which kind of person we should want to be.

I don't know why Dallas Willard works so hard to shift the Beatitudes from something we're called to live toward. Especially in light of what is otherwise a wonderful book about really following Jesus and not just making empty confessions of belief.

When I first read *The Divine Conspiracy*, I was so excited reading the first several chapters, I underlined and highlighted almost half of what Willard wrote: *"The practical irrelevance of actual obedience to Christ* accounts for the weakened effect of Christianity in the world today [emph. his]" (p. xv). He says on the following page that he assumes one doesn't need to be a late twentieth-century scholar to understand the Bible's meaning. He critiques a Christianity with a primary emphasis on what he calls "sin management" and preparing for the next life with little emphasis on this life. So that "being a Christian then comes to have nothing to do with the kind of person one is" (p. 56).

Willard assumes we can trust that Jesus was indeed wise and competent enough to show and teach us a way of life that really works in the world. Jesus was not naïve, mistaken, hapless, or ignorant. Yet he notes that

> the disappearance of Jesus as a teacher [which] explains why today in Christian churches, of whatever leaning, little effort is made to teach people to do what he did and taught. . . . We do not seriously consider Jesus as our teacher on how to live, hence we cannot think of ourselves, in our moment-to-moment existence, as his students or disciples. So we turn to popular speakers and writers, some Christian and some not—whoever happens to be writing books and running talk shows and seminars on matters that concern us. The disconnection of life from faith, the absence from our churches of Jesus the teacher . . . is largely caused and sustained by the basic message that we constantly hear from Christ-

ian pulpits . . . with what I have called "gospels of sin management," while Jesus' invitation to eternal life now . . . remains for the most part ignored and unspoken. (p. 57)

On the next page Willard adds, "To counteract this we must develop a straightforward presentation, in word and life, of the reality of life now under God's rule."

I was so excited to read this challenge to actually teach and discuss and put into practice what Jesus taught. So I was doubly baffled by the dismissal of the Beatitudes as pointing to a Christian ethic or mindset or attitude. Willard was heavy on having an attitude of trust in God but light on actual applications from Jesus' teachings.

On the whole I recommend this wonderful book. I just find his take on the Sermon on the Mount and especially the Beatitudes to be tortured interpretations, contradicting the inspiring things he says about trusting in Jesus and actually following him.

APPENDIX 2

Albert Nolan, a Christian scholar, suggests Jesus was more genuinely concerned about liberation than the Zealots were.

> They wanted a mere change of government—from Roman to Jewish. Jesus wanted a change that . . . would reach down to the most basic assumption of Jew and Roman. Jesus wanted a qualitatively different world—the kingdom of God. (*Jesus Before Christianity*, pp. 116-117)

To replace one worldly government with another would be no liberation at all for the poor and oppressed. "Jesus saw what no one else had been able to see, that there was more oppression and economic exploitation from within Judaism than from without." The middle-class, educated Jews—the scribes, Pharisees, Sadducees, and Zealots who were in rebellion against Rome were themselves oppressors of the poor and uneducated.

> The real issue was oppression itself and not the fact that a pagan Roman dared to oppress God's chosen people. The root cause of oppression was man's lack of compassion. Those who resented Roman oppression but overlooked their own oppression of the poor

were lacking in compassion just as much as, if not more than, the Romans. (p. 118)

Jesus wanted to bring about a far more radical revolution than the Zealots had in mind. They were fighting for Jewish nationalism and Jewish ethnicity. Jesus wanted a genuine liberation for all people that transformed every sphere of life—political, economic, social, and religious. He showed that the current ideas of what was just and right were loveless, lacking in compassion, and therefore contrary to the will of God.

> We find examples of this in the parable of the laborers in the vineyard (Mt 20:1-15) and in the parable of the prodigal son (Luke 15:11-32). The laborers who have done "a heavy days work in all the heat" complain because others have received the same wages for working only one hour. . . . But the employer, like God, had been moved by compassion . . . and paid them a wage which was not proportionate to the work done but proportionate to their needs. . . . Those who worked all day do not share their employer's compassion for the others and therefore complain. Their "justice" like the "justice" of the Zealots and Pharisees, is loveless. They envy the good fortune of others and, like Jonah, they regret God's compassion and generosity toward others. (p. 119)

Nolan goes on to say that the elder son in the story of the prodigal son is indignant at the fathers' forgiveness and joy over his returned son. Jesus did not accuse the Zealots and Pharisees of being too political but of being too religious. Their religious fanaticism is what led them to kill pagan intruders and Jews who collaborated with them. Religious fanaticism led the Pharisees to persecute and oppress the poor and the sinners and caused the Essenes' hatred of unclean Jews and Gentiles.

> One of the basic causes of oppression, discrimination, and suffering in that society was its religion—the loveless religion of the Pharisees, Sadducees, Es-

senes, and Zealots. And nothing is more impervious
to change than religious zeal. (p. 120)

The religious leaders looked forward with anticipation
to the coming of the Messiah which they assumed would put
them back on top as the rightful leaders of Israel. They
worked harder and prepared more diligently for his coming
than other folks. But Jesus' agenda wasn't at all what they
prepared for. They expected to be affirmed for being so serious and committed to studying and applying the Scriptures.
But Jesus looked at the Scripture in surprising ways—far less
committed to the rules and far more committed to loving
people despite their brokenness.

Jesus' social agenda was based on acceptance, forgiveness, and inclusion rather than the Pharisee's agenda of purity and separation from "unclean and unholy" people.
Jesus' primary guiding principle was compassion; theirs was
holiness.

REFERENCES

Allen, James and John Littlefield. *Without Sanctuary*. Santa Fe, N.M.: Twin Palms Publishers, 2000.

Augsburger, David. "The Mennonite Dream," Elkhart, Ind.: Mennonite Board of Missions, 1970.

DeMars, Gary. *End Times Fiction*. Nashville: Thomas Nelson, 2001.

Drury, Keith. "Who Says What The Bible Says? The Keys to the Kingdom, Binding and Loosing." Christian Resource Institute, *The Voice*, online at http://www.crivoice.org/bindloose.html, 2011.

Ehrman, Bart D. *Misquoting Jesus*. New York: Harper Collins Publishers, 2005.

Goldhagen, Daniel Jonah. *Hitler's Willing Executioners*. New York: Alfred A. Knopf, 1996.

Guthrie, Stan. "Foolish Things: When Red is Blue—Why I'm not a Red Letter Christian." *Christianity Today*, October 2007, 100.

Guthrie, Stan. "Grace as a License to Sin, Stan Guthrie interviews Robert Jeffress." *Christianity Today,* March 2006, 76.

Kinnaman, David and Gabe Lyons. *unChristian.* Grand Rapids, Mich.: Baker Books, 2007.

Lewis, C. S. "Why I Am Not a Pacifist." In *The Weight of Glory and Other Essays.* HarperCollins, 1980, 64-90.

Meachum, Jon. "The God Debate," interview with Rick Warren and Sam Harris. *Newsweek,* April 9, 2007, 63.

Miller, Donald. *Blue Like Jazz.* Nashville: Thomas Nelson Publishers, 2003.

Nolen, Albert. *Jesus Before Christianity.* Maryknoll, N.Y.: Orbis Books, 2007

Palmer, Parker J. *Let Your Life Speak.* San Francisco: Jossey-Bass, 2000.

Stobie, Thomas A, S.F.O. "Being Poor in Spirit." Online at: stobie.home.sprynet.com/religion/PoorInSpirit.htm. 2002-8.

Willard, Dallas. *The Divine Conspiracy: Rediscovering Our Hidden Life In God.* Harper San Francisco, 1998.

THE AUTHOR

Duane Beachey is currently a pastor who has spent most of his life working to improve housing for low-income families in Oklahoma City, San Antonio, Texas, and in southeastern Kentucky. He lives with his wife Gloria in Isom, Kentucky, where, although he is an ordained Mennonite pastor, he is pastoring two small Presbyterian churches in Isom and Blackey, Kentucky.

Much of his life Beachey has worked across denominational lines with an interfaith housing organization in Oklahoma, and with an interfaith peace organization he helped form—Oklahoma Peace Strategies. Beachey then worked with Habitat for Humanity in Oklahoma and Texas. He served as pastor of the San Antonio Mennonite Church for eight years. Most recently he and his wife Gloria completed eight years of service with Mennonite Central Committee coordinating MCC's work in Appalachia.

Beachey is author of *Faith in a Nuclear Age* (Herald Press, 1983). After growing up in Arthur, Illinois, Beachey attended college in Hesston, Kansas, and Goshen, Indiana. He attended one year at the Associated (now Anabaptist) Mennonite Biblical Seminary in 1973-74.

Duane and Gloria have two daughters, three grandsons, and a granddaughter.